"Gregg Jantz has once again used wise, biblical insights to shed light on our love affair with behaviors that give us short-term thrills at the expense of long-term healing. This book could help restore sanity and serenity to gamblers and other hard-core risktakers who are tired of living too close to the edge."

—Pat Means, president of Prodigals International
and author of *Men's Secret Wars*

"This book brings hope, healing, and the possibility of a healthy life for those who suffer and practical ways to help for those who care. I highly recommend it and encourage you to read it now."

—Rich Hurst, pastor, author, and director of Strategic Adult
Ministry, Cook Communication Ministry

"The gambling trap ensnares increasing numbers of unsuspecting men and women. *Turning the Tables on Gambling* makes good sense and offers hope to those who have found themselves falling into a lifestyle of speculation rather than reality."

—Jim Hayford Sr., senior pastor, Eastside Foursquare Church,
Seattle, Washington

"Compulsive gambling is a killer disease. This brilliant, well-written book will help many."

—Dr. Bruce Larson, pastor emeritus University Presbyterian
Church, Seattle, and author of twenty-three books

TURNING

the TABLES _on_

GAMBLING

Hope and Help for an Addictive Behavior

GREGORY L. JANTZ

with ANN McMURRAY

SHAW

WATERBROOK
PRESS

Turning the Tables on Gambling
A SHAW BOOK
PUBLISHED BY WATERBROOK PRESS
2375 Telstar Drive, Suite 160
Colorado Springs, Colorado 80920
A division of Random House, Inc.

Some of the stories in this book are composites of several different situations; details and names have been changed to protect identities.

Unless otherwise noted, Scripture quotations are taken from the *Holy Bible, New International Version*®. NIV® Copyright © 1973, 1978, 1984 by International Bible Society. Used by permission of Zondervan Publishing House. All rights reserved. Scriptures marked (NASB) are taken from the *New American Standard Bible*®. © Copyright The Lockman Foundation 1960, 1962, 1963, 1968, 1971, 1972, 1973, 1975, 1977, 1995. Used by permission. (www.Lockman.org)

ISBN 0-87788-301-7

Library of Congress Cataloging-in-Publication Data
Jantz, Gregory L.
    Turning the tables on gambling : hope and help for an addictive behavior / Gregory L. Jantz with Ann McMurray.
      p. cm.
    ISBN 0-87788-301-7 (paper)
      1. Gambling.   2. Gambling—Religious aspects—Christianity.   3. Compulsive gamblers—Rehabilitation.   I. McMurray, Ann.   II. Title.

    HV6713 .J36 2001
    362.2'5—dc21
                                                            00-050976

Printed in the United States of America
2001—First Shaw Edition

10 9 8 7 6 5 4 3 2 1

*To the countless individuals and families
suffering in the silent despair of the grasp of gambling—
may there be hope in these pages to make a true turn
in the turning of the tables.*

Becoming Strong Again

Healing the Scars of Emotional Abuse

Hidden Dangers of the Internet: Using It Without Abusing It

Hope, Help, and Healing for Eating Disorders: A New Approach for Treating Anorexia, Bulimia, and Overeating

Losing Weight Permanently: Secrets of the 2% Who Succeed

The Spiritual Path to Weight Loss

Too Close to the Flame: Recognizing and Avoiding Sexualized Relationships

Twenty-One Days to Better Eating

CONTENTS

ACKNOWLEDGMENTS

This important work was possible because of the blessing, belief, and effort of our team. Our gratitude to Joan Guest, Elisa Fryling, Carol Bartley, Don Pape, and all our new friends at WaterBrook. It was the writing talents and skills of Ann McMurray that gave life to these pages. Thank you, Ann, for the blessing of our team.

—Gregg

I would like to acknowledge my family—Tad, Joel, Lindsay, and Jason—whose love makes each day a blessing.

—Ann

INTRODUCTION

Twenty years ago the words *Christian* and *gambling* together would probably have produced a mental picture of a church basement with chipped tables, metal folding chairs, a spinning cage, and the sound of "Bingo!" ringing out.

Twenty years ago if Christians wanted to gamble legally outside of that basement, they needed to live in a state with a horse track, dog track, or lottery, and there weren't many.

Twenty years ago if Christians wanted to play the slots or try their luck at blackjack or poker, they needed to board a plane, train, or automobile and travel to a Las Vegas casino.

Times have changed.

In June 1997 the federal government, responding to pressure from concerned citizens and members of Congress, commissioned a two-year study to look at the growth of gambling and to begin to delineate the effects of gambling on the United States and its citizens. The last federal study on the effects of gambling had been completed over twenty years earlier, in 1976, and in the interim, gambling across the country and on Native American tribal lands had exploded.

In July 1999 the National Gambling Impact Study Commission (NGISC) finished and delivered its report. Kay C. James, chairman of the commission, presented the report to the president, Congress, governors, and tribal leaders. Within its pages was a frank evaluation of the current state of gambling and how gambling had changed from 1976 to 1997. The commission did extensive research and visited a variety of gambling venues from around the country: casinos in Atlantic City, New Jersey; lotteries in Boston, Massachusetts; riverboat casinos in Chicago, Illinois; Indian gambling and pari-mutuel betting in San Diego, California, and Tempe, Arizona; casinos in Biloxi, Mississippi, and New Orleans, Louisiana; and sports betting, casinos, and other forms of casino-style gambling in Las Vegas, Nevada. While the amount of available data on gambling was small, the choice of gambling venues to review was extensive.

According to the report from the NGISC, "the gambling industry in the United States has grown tenfold since 1975. Today a person can make a legal wager of some sort in every state except Utah, Tennessee, and Hawaii. Thirty-seven states and the District of Columbia have lotteries, 28 states authorized casino gambling and 43 states have pari-mutuel betting."[1] The growth of the gambling industry in the United States is undeniable, but how does this affect the average American?

WHEN GAMBLING IS ALL AROUND

The significance of the past twenty years, I believe, is not how much people have moved toward gambling, but how much gambling has moved toward people. Gambling has moved in, literally, to our very doorsteps. Along Main Street and in corner grocery stores, Christians daily face increased opportunities to gamble. Governmental agencies have replaced business as the prime providers of gambling in many locations, using the enormous resources at their disposal to promote this activity. The need to travel to a destination in order to gamble has been obliterated by the onset of Internet gambling, taking gambling-style gaming into dens, bedrooms, and kitchens across this country.

What about Christians? How have Christians reacted to this upswing in gambling choices? According to research by the Barna

Group, Christians are indistinguishable from society in a wide range of behaviors, including gambling. Roughly a quarter of the general population purchases a lottery ticket during the course of a week, and Christians are no different.[2] Though no comprehensive study exists outlining a correlation between gambling and people of the Christian faith, research done by Harvard Medical School indicates over 15 million people display some sign of a gambling addiction.[3] In the seventeen states conducting surveys, an estimated 1.7 to 7.3 percent of the adult population exhibits problem or pathological tendencies in their gambling behaviors.[4] Most assuredly there are Christians trapped among that growing group.

What is the distinction of being a Christian if Christians succumb to gambling just like everyone else? Aren't Christians supposed to be somehow special and insulated from compulsions? The answer to the first part of that last question is yes, Christians are set apart by their special relationship with God. However, the answer to the second part of the question is not so clear-cut. Christians are not automatically free from sin and addictive behaviors, as the book of First John makes clear. John writes, "If we claim to be without sin, we deceive ourselves and the truth is not in us" (1 John 1:8). None of us is completely isolated from this world and its effects.

WHERE DO WE DRAW THE LINE?

We live in the midst of a time increasingly comfortable with gambling as a concept and increasingly tolerant of an expanding number of gambling venues. I believe the question for Christians is, how comfortable should we be with gambling? When, for example, is it okay to wager with a buddy for a Coke after a softball game? Is it all right for Christians to place a bet on a horse race or buy a lottery ticket or play nickel-ante cards at a friend's house?

Where is the line for the Christian and when has it been crossed? Is it going to Las Vegas three times a year instead of once? Is it buying a lottery ticket once a week instead of once a month? Is it playing video poker over the Internet? Is it only a problem if you don't have the money to lose?

These are complex issues that require an honest appraisal by every person who reads this book. I applaud your desire to learn more about how gambling affects lives in general and Christians in particular. For a line does exist in gambling. On one side is a neutral, recreational activity enjoyed by millions of Americans every year. On the other side is a compulsive, destructive behavior that affects a small but significant few.

Throughout this book, the terms *compulsive, problem,* and *pathological* will be used to define gambling behaviors that have crossed over the line from recreational to destructive. The American Psychiatric Association's Diagnostic and Statistical Manual provides a straightforward measure of that line when it states, "Compulsive or pathological gambling is a progressive behavior disorder in which an individual has a psychologically uncontrollable preoccupation with and urge to gamble that compromises family, occupational and other pursuits." In other words, gambling is compulsive when it controls life rather than contributes to life.

THE REASONS FOR THIS BOOK

The spread of gambling is a recent cultural phenomenon, and the effects of gambling are just beginning to come to the surface. The question of gambling's influence is moving out of a clinical realm and into the culture's awareness. Now, not only are psychiatrists and psychologists asking questions about the impacts of gambling, society is too. We are noticing the overwhelming impact of gambling, and we are beginning to ask what, if anything, can be done to help. More and more people are being confronted with the negative results of gambling in their own lives and in the lives of those around them.

This cultural conversation is swelling in volume. As the federal government contends with the results of the NGISC, states are evaluating whether the money generated by state-sanctioned gambling is worth the cost to their citizenry. Communities wrestle with civic decisions about whether to allow gambling within their borders as individuals look at themselves, their loved ones, and the effects of personal gambling behaviors.

The Voice of Hope

This book is written to add a Christian perspective to society's conversations about gambling. In the cultural discussion, Christians add the voice of hope. Those who become trapped in gambling have a powerful God who is able to rescue them and pull them up from the pit of their destructive behavior. As the psalmist tells us, God is the one who "redeems your life from the pit" (Psalm 103:4).

Make no mistake: Problem gambling is a compulsion leading to a pit. It wrecks finances, strains occupations, devastates relationships. It invites other addictive behaviors to join it, from alcoholism to sexual immorality. It takes center stage in the gambler's life, eventually crowding out everything else, including God. The pull of this pit is strong. Only through the power of God in the Holy Spirit will the compulsive gambler be rescued.

For twenty years gambling has been gaining momentum, propelling people over the line into compulsion. This book is written to help you answer the questions, "Where is my line where gambling is concerned?" "What do I do if I've already crossed that line?" "How do I help someone else who has crossed that line?" This book is written to give practical help and concrete hope.

The Voice of Truth

The gambling industry does not want any part of its activities to be viewed as a pit. It tries very hard to craft and maintain an image of carefree fun, excitement, and escape from reality. Along with its willing partners in government, the gambling industry seeks to downplay gambling's dangers and marginalize those who fall prey to compulsive gambling behaviors. Gambling is harmless to most, the industry claims, and only a few people—an acceptably small number of people—have problems with it. The industry consistently places its money where its mouth is, pumping in advertising dollars to businesses and providing tax revenues to governments. The voice of gambling is loud.

This book is written to turn the tables on gambling, to examine the truth of what gambling promises against what it actually delivers. This book is written to uncover the truth about gambling—its effects on people and how their struggles affect us all.

PERSONAL, CULTURAL, SPIRITUAL

You will find this book is divided into three sections. Section 1 looks at those individuals and personalities most at risk for problem gambling. Gambling is a neutral activity in and of itself. One person can gamble without losing control; another cannot gamble with control. The activity is the same, so what makes the two persons different?

Section 2 discusses the cultural aspects of gambling. Gambling, as it is presented today, is a result of societal decisions. True, each person who gambles must make an individual choice about whether or not to gamble, but our society has also made decisions about what types of gambling to accept and promote. This section will take an in-depth look at how our culture supports the gambling lifestyle, the changes made in the gambling industry over the past twenty years, and what those changes have meant.

Section 3 is the voice of hope. This section will give you practical help if you gamble occasionally or if you struggle with a more serious gambling addiction. It will also offer suggestions for the person wanting to help a friend or loved one who gambles. We will look at what God has to say about gambling, money, and the lifestyle choices of his children. God is not surprised by the choices people make. He is not oblivious to the society we have created for ourselves. The devastating effects of compulsive gambling are not a modern-day phenomenon, catching God unaware. The cultural conversation may have just gotten started, but God has always had the answer. After people have made their choices and the culture has had its say, the last word is God's. What is that last word? Hope.

Part of receiving that hope is realizing where we need help. Following each section is a list of questions that will help you look at your own needs, behaviors, and perceptions and the needs and behaviors of others around you. These follow-up guides can be used for individual reflection as well as group discussion. You will also find a self-evaluation questionnaire in Appendix C. These questions will help you evaluate your gambling behaviors or the gambling behaviors of someone you care about. It might be helpful for you to take this test at several different points as you read this book. Your answers may change as you read.

Joining this journey to hope will require courage. Few voices in society today warn us about problem gambling and its devastating consequences. On the contrary, one of the strongest voices in our society—government—is using its power to promote gambling as a way to increase revenue. Indeed, culture itself in its preoccupation with wealth provides a constant siren song of materialism, luring people into a headlong pursuit of financial reward. Society, with its momentum permanently stuck on fast forward, propels the myth of instant gratification with financial freedom just a lottery ticket away. Taken together, these forces create a tremendous undertow seeking to suck us down into the pit of compulsive gambling.

As strong as these voices are today, God's voice is more powerful. His message is clear and consistent. His help is unassailable and accessible. His presence is promised and persistent. There is no place you can go, from the cathedral to the casino, where God is not present. He is with us in the pit of compulsion, giving us strength to get out; he is with us in our relationships as we wonder how we can help someone else get out of that pit. His words to Joshua in the Old Testament are still true: "Be strong and courageous. Do not be terrified; do not be discouraged, for the LORD your God will be with you wherever you go" (Joshua 1:9). God is with us on this journey to find healing, answers, and freedom.

This truly is hope.

SECTION 1

THE HAND THAT ROLLS THE DICE

Gambling is not an activity that occurs by itself. Someone must place the bet, roll the dice, pull the lever, buy the ticket. Not everyone does these things; over a third of the adult population in this country did not place a bet of any kind in the past year.[1] But close to two-thirds of the population did, and for some it wasn't just a casual bet or a whimsical wager on winning the latest lottery. For some, gambling isn't recreation, it's life—life that has taken on a shape and scope all its own.

Since Christians are drawn to gambling at about the same rate as the general population, it is important to look at the following questions:

- Who, in the general population, is gambling and why?
- What are the forces drawing people to gamble for the first time?
- What are the forces compelling them to return again and again?
- If the consequences of problem gambling are so devastating, why would people continue in such a destructive behavior?
- What needs, if any, are being addressed through gambling behaviors?

Each chapter in this section will introduce you to a specific gambler. After a short profile that summarizes the characteristics of each type of gambler, the rest of the chapter will discuss the motivations and reasons behind gambling behavior. (Remember as you read that we will get to practical suggestions for helping these gambling behaviors in section 3.)

The profiles are not necessarily of Christians, but the motivations and reasons for their gambling need to be examined by Christians. As you look at the personality of the gambler, honestly evaluate yourself to see how your attitudes and motivations might be "meshing" with those of the world. Take the time to answer the self-evaluation questions at the end of this section. You may be surprised at how many of these attitudes and motivations affect you, even if you don't gamble yourself.

JUST FOR THRILLS

Steve remembers vividly the cacophony of sights and sounds that greeted his entry into the casino for the first time. It was deliciously chaotic, with lights flashing and bells and whistles going off in every direction. Things were happening. Exciting things. He couldn't wait to wade into the middle of it all and be lifted on the swell of the tide. Two of his buddies who had been there before started moving toward the blackjack tables, pulling out the cash in their pockets and motioning for him to catch up. Oh, he caught up all right.

Caught up and passed them. By the end of the night, both of his friends had lost about two hundred bucks a piece, but Steve was ahead more than a thousand dollars. Steve could close his eyes and play back in his mind that first big win. They'd been gambling at blackjack for several hours, with pots changing hands back and forth between those seated at the table and the house dealer. One of his friends, having already lost all of his money, was sitting it out, watching the action from the sidelines. The heat of the action caused a small eddy in the stream of gamblers flowing around the casino, with several onlookers caught up in the backwater of their play. Round and round they went, raising and calling, raising and calling, until three players at the table just kept raising the stakes. No one seemed willing to call, each sure of his own hand.

Sweat rolling down his neck and back, Steve doggedly hung on even though his friend was flashing signs of concern in his direction.

The pot represented a lot of money, weeks of work for any of them. After numerous circuits around the table, Steve's other friend dropped out, but Steve remained. Heart pumping, he felt terrified and intensely alive. The risk involved in losing that much money was almost unbearable. Almost unbearable—and unbelievably exciting. This, Steve thought to himself in the midst of it all, is an absolute kick.

There was no telling what Steve would have thought if he'd lost, because he didn't. He won the pot, with his friends letting out whoops of joy and pounding on his back gleefully. Steve could still remember how great he'd felt looking at all that money, his money, lying on the table.

The Thrill of Victory

Like Steve, close to half of problem gamblers trace their gambling compulsion back to a big win.[1] The euphoria of that win is so significant, it drives the individual to continually repeat the gambling activity in order to experience the risk-thrill cycle all over again.

Gambling is certainly not the only high-risk activity producing a euphoric thrill. People have always engaged in behaviors that are extremely dangerous yet rewarding. Every four years the world pauses to watch its best athletes compete in racing down a frosty mountain at tremendous speeds. Or corkscrewing through a twisting track of ice on nothing but a slender sled. Or flying off the end of a multistory ramp over packed snow. Skydiving, racecar driving, and bungee jumping are similar types of activity. They all involve a high level of risk and a distinct physical reaction during the experience.

This physical reaction is called a "rush." Indeed, it is a rush of adrenaline produced by the body as part of the "fight or flight" response. This rush of adrenaline causes the heart to pump faster and the lungs to work harder, increasing oxygen to the blood. Heightened senses, easily interpreted and responded to, produce crisp and clear sights and sounds. The body prepares in this state of emergency in case the person needs to either fight or take flight. When the rush is produced, the body does not differentiate between a real life-threatening situation and a high-risk activity.

Some people observe high-risk activities and see only the risk, not the rush. The threat of injury isn't thrilling, it's terrifying. Heart pumping, palms sweating, breath racing, this heightened adrenal state is viewed negatively. The very thought of doing something so risky that it produces these physical changes scares some people to death, and they do whatever they can to avoid it.

Some people observe high-risk activities and see only the rush, downplaying the risk. These people are thrill seekers. The physical reaction, the rush of adrenaline, is highly desirable to the thrill seeker. Drawn to it, he* seeks out activities and behaviors that produce its euphoric thrill.

For the thrill-seeker personality, however, the euphoric thrill does not occur only at the end of the high-risk activity. Even the act of risk produces the euphoria, whether or not the goal is actually accomplished at the end of the activity. The activity itself is invigorating. In fact, it may be the only time the thrill seeker feels invigorated. In other words, only during times of intense stress does the thrill-seeker personality feel truly alive.

MANUFACTURED CRISES

These times of stress are actually manufactured crises. In the case of high-risk sports activities, only training and physical prowess can successfully extricate the athlete from the risk of injury or defeat. The question of that outcome is why spectators exist. Will they win? Will they lose? How well will each player fare? Defeat as well as victory compels people to watch. It is not, after all, only the amazing catches or spectacular dunks that make the highlight films. It is also the high-speed crashes and the bone-jarring falls. The drama of a manufactured crisis is the essence of the thrill of

---

*Masculine and feminine pronouns will alternate by chapter.

sports. Sports itself is a high-stakes affair because of the enormous salaries paid, the rewards of winning, and the negative results of losing.

For the gambler, the manufactured crisis is the wager. It is manufactured because the wager is completely voluntary. No outside force compels the gambler to place the bet or make the wager. It is a crisis because of the consequences of losing. The higher the monetary risk, the greater the crisis.

All of us must weather crises, but most people have no desire to perpetually live in them. We recognize that even crisis moments have positive components, such as clarifying priorities or emphasizing the value of family and friends. We appreciate the calm at the end of the storm as an opportunity to recoup and solidify the lessons learned. The furnace of crisis has value, but most of us don't want to continually live in that heat.

The thrill seeker doesn't know how to live without the heat. He feels empty, not relieved, at the end of a crisis. Compared to the Technicolor intensity present during the crisis, real life is pale and washed out. With nothing on the line, real life is meaningless and without value.

Gambling activities are extremely compelling to the thrill seeker, especially those without the athletic prowess or coordination necessary to engage in high-risk physical activities. Gambling produces the same level of risk and thrill of the manufactured crisis in sports, without requiring the participant to be athletically inclined. In fact, sometimes gambling behaviors supplant athletic activities as the thrill seeker ages and loses his physical edge.

ALL OR NOTHING

Why would anyone want to live in such a heightened state all the time? Because the thrill seeker doesn't think there is any other way to live. When not in the midst of a crisis, his life feels like nothing. But this is not a normal way to look at life; circumstances have conditioned the thrill seeker to desire the intensity of the crisis. As a child, he may have grown up in living situations where crises occurred regularly through the addictive behaviors of a parent or other adult. This addictive behavior could have been alcoholism, a drug habit, or even gambling. Whatever the behavior of the adult, it produced a crisis that then affected the child.

During crisis times involving the adult, different conditions emerged that the child interpreted as desirable. On the one hand, during the crisis the child may be called upon to operate as the adult, making decisions with the appearance of being in control. This role reversal during crisis, of adult-to-child and child-to-adult, produces feelings of power and control in the child. The upheaval at the onset of the crisis brings about initial feelings of loss of control (risk), but the role reversal during the crisis helps the child feel he is regaining that control (thrill).

On the other hand, during the crisis the adult may ignore the child completely. At times such as these, the child may be left on his own, unprotected, with the adult abdicating any overt control (risk). Without adult oversight, the child is left to operate free of restraint (thrill).

In either case, the child interprets the advent of crises as an opportunity for control. This control is made all the more important by the persistent out-of-control behavior of the adult. Feeling in control during the crisis, the child attempts to impose order on himself or others in the family.

Over time the child is drawn into the cycle of risk-thrill. At the onset of the crisis, the risk for the child was multiple. Will he gain control over the situation? Will control bring about positive or negative results? Times of crisis mean heightened activity, awareness, decision making, and control. By contrast, the child comes to interpret the times between each crisis negatively. No longer in crisis, the child reverts back to a submissive role under the control of the unreliable adult.

This flat state between crises pales in comparison to the thrill of crises. Eventually even the noncrisis state is not entirely flat. For between each crisis, the next crisis is building, the risk factor incrementally increasing. The child never knows when the next crisis will occur or the severity of that crisis when it arrives. The child doesn't like this between time as much as the assured pattern and timing of the actual crisis. Crisis mode becomes the preferred state.

Thrill seekers are often adult children of continual crisis. What most people find uncomfortable and exhausting, the thrill seeker finds familiar and invigorating. Rather than avoid risky behaviors, the thrill seeker engages in behaviors that produce crises. Gambling, with its manufactured crises, is tailor-made for this personality.

Not all the childhood situations reinforcing the thrill-seeker personality involve substance abuse or addictive adult behaviors. Crises occur in families for many reasons. A job change, a death in the family, a physical move, and difficulties with other family members can all produce family crises. Some families are simply more prone to crises than others. The difference is in how the adults in the family manage the crisis and what that teaches their children.

Crises can also occur in families because of the emotional state of an adult in the family. Some adults produce family crises by their intense mood swings and emotional imbalance through depression, hyperactivity, or a combination of the two. In such a case there is no outside influence or substance. Whatever the case, the potential for producing the thrill-seeker personality is the same.

This is not to say that only childhood situations produce thrill-seeker personalities. As some people progress into adulthood they adopt a thrill-seeker personality based on adult circumstances. It may take only one event to trigger a desire to repeat the risk-thrill cycle in adults. Intense gambling situations can provide such an event.

T Is for *Thrill* and *Testosterone*

Psychologist Frank Farley has advanced the proposition that there are "Big T" personalities, with the *T* standing for *thrill* and *testosterone*. In an article in *Psychology Today,* Farley outlines the Big T as a thrill-seeker personality because of a need, dating back to infancy, for a high level of stimulation. This increased need for stimulation has its root in "a person's biological, possibly genetic, makeup. Experiences around the time of birth or perhaps early nutrition may also play a part."[2] Farley identifies this person as predominantly male and young, around sixteen to twenty-four years old. (His article also includes a detailed section on how this personality affects women.) According to Farley, Big Ts prefer uncertainty, unpredictability, high risk, novelty, variety, complexity, ambiguity, flexibility, low structure, high intensity, and high conflict.

What does the Big T personality do with this need for stimulation? When thrill seekers use the need constructively, they become entertainers, entrepreneurs, or sports heroes. When the need is used destructively, Big T personalities can become criminals.[3]

The danger for gamblers with this type of profile is twofold. The need for stimulation may draw the Big T personality into gambling. When his gambling becomes a significant monetary drain, though, his personality may make him more prone to criminal behavior. This criminal behavior is a high-intensity, high-risk way to make up for gambling losses or to provide money to continue gambling.

STRIKING A BALANCE

However the thrill-seeker personality was formed, it must be recognized as an inappropriate response to life. The pursuit of extraordinary stimulation through risk-thrill behaviors should not overwhelm the routine activities of living. It is not healthy to view everyday life as drab and unfulfilling. It is not healthy to engage in high-risk, destructive behaviors as a way to feel alive. It is not healthy to elevate excitement or thrill above common sense or appropriate caution. Even the desire for thrill or stimulation can be channeled into positive, constructive activities that add to, not detract from, life.

There is nothing wrong with being excited, even ecstatic. This state is achieved without harm every day. Who hasn't cheered a school's team on to victory? Who hasn't let out a whoop of joy when a sporting team wins a big event or spent hours watching Olympic slalom, luge, or ski-jumping events? There is certainly nothing wrong in engaging in most sporting activities, even so-called high-risk sports, if we are properly prepared to face the challenge. There may be nothing psychologically damaging with using disposable income to purchase a lottery ticket or place a wager on a horse race for recreation. Millions of people do so every day with no ill effects. The danger is that these activities and the thrill they bring can quickly become a substitute for life. Without healthy motivation and moderation, these activities don't augment life, they control it.

FOR THE LOVE OF MONEY

Relief flooded Janice. She couldn't even call it excitement or thrill, just overwhelming relief. She'd won, really won, after seven hours straight, switching back and forth between her "lucky" bank of slots. She laughed ironically to herself at the thought of these being a "bank" of slots. They were her bank, to be sure. Every dime had gone right back into them over the course of the evening. Each time she won a small amount, she pumped those coins back in, hoping, praying for more.

Now the gamble had paid off. Lights flashed, whistles whooped, and coins clinked and clanked, scatter-shot, down onto the metal tray. Numbly she began scooping them into the coin cup she'd been working on all night. A casino employee came over and provided additional cups when hers became full. Other gamblers looked at her with a mixture of excitement and envy. Janice was too relieved to care about the lights and the noise and the stares. All she cared about was scooping up those coins and getting to the cashier's window without losing any along the way.

Bills were due, most of them overdue. She'd gone through a bad streak lately, and paychecks evaporated before Janice could even get them to the bank. Truth was, quite a bit of her last several paychecks was in the "bank" she'd just walked away from. Crossing the casino floor, Janice calculated in her mind which bills she'd pay off, which bills she'd pay down, and which bills she could ignore for a few more weeks.

After all, she couldn't use it all for bills. Her sister was nagging her about the money she owed her for watching the kids. She hadn't really gone to the grocery store for more than the bare necessities in…well, she couldn't remember how long. She still owed a lot of money to pay overdue utilities bills, to say nothing of the credit cards. The bills together were overwhelming and a lot more than she'd won. So some of this had to be left for next time. After all, it took money to make money, and Janice knew it wouldn't be long before she'd be back at the slots, trying to do it all over again.

HOUSE ADVANTAGE

The gambling industry is not a charity and would never refer to itself as such. It does refer to itself as gaming, entertainment, or part of the recreation or leisure industry. Whatever the term, its main business is making money, taking money. The gambling industry takes money from gamblers like Janice all of the time, gives a portion back to some gamblers in winnings part of the time, and keeps most of the money for itself. How much money? In 1997 gambling profits in casinos equaled more than $30 billion,[1] while state lotteries profited by almost $17 billion.[2] With billions of dollars in profit, some gamblers may be winning money, but most are losing.

How much are they losing? For the great majority of gamblers tracked at casinos, the amount of money lost was relatively small. The 1999 National Gambling Impact Study Commission reported that casinos "estimated that more than a third of their gambling revenue was generated by players whose gambling losses were less than $100 annually, with more than half of revenues from players whose gambling losses amounted to less than $500 annually."[3] This still leaves over 15 percent of revenues generated by problem gamblers whose losses spiral upward toward the significant and the potentially devastating.

This 15 percent figure has been disputed by some as too low. A Focus on the Family Research Report based on the NGISC study says,

"Dr. Henry Lesieur calculated that problem and pathological gamblers account for an average of 30.4 percent of total gambling expenditures in the 4 U.S. states and 3 Canadian provinces he examined."[4] The report goes on to say: "other recent studies at the state level provide further evidence [of the 15 percent figure being too low]. A 1998 study commissioned by the state of Montana found that problem and pathological gamblers account for 36 percent of electronic gambling device (EGD) revenues, 28 percent of live keno expenditures, and 18 percent of lottery scratch ticket sales."[5] A 1999 Louisiana study found that this problem population of gamblers accounted for "30 percent of all spending on riverboat casinos, 42 percent of Indian casino spending, and 27 percent on expenditures of EGD machines."[6] As these figures suggest, problem gambling is likely a more common problem than we initially imagined.

THE GAMBLING POOR

Regardless of what study is used, compulsive gamblers are losing incredible amounts of money in order to continue their behavior. The statistics may come with sanitized terms like *percent,* but those numbers represent people who are trapped in their gambling addictions. Whatever compelled them to begin gambling, they seem helpless to stop. The more they gamble, the more they lose, draining their own resources and becoming the gambling poor.

According to information on problem gambling, after the thrill of the big win inevitably comes the losing phase.[7] It is during this losing phase that problem gamblers begin to pile up losses, straining their finances and self-esteem. No longer in control of gambling, gambling takes control of them.

Relationships with family members and friends cease their traditional meaning as the gambler looks at others primarily as a source for additional funds. Stray acquaintances can be asked for money. Even without the actual funds to gamble, the gambler is consumed with thoughts of gambling. When money is obtained, gambling will continue.

Why would someone financially strapped by gambling losses continue to gamble? Why doesn't she recognize gambling as the source of monetary drain and stop? The answer comes through two words—false hope. In the desperation to win and recoup her losses, the gambler is blinded by the false hope of the next big strike.

Disregarding the losses, the gambler views the lightning flash of luck as proof of the need to continue to gamble. In the gambler's mind, all that is needed is for lightning to strike twice. She knows she can win again because she's won before. Gambling got her into this situation, and gambling will get her out.

So sure is the gambler of winning, she continues to pump more and more dollars into gambling. Winning is, of course, inevitable. Gambling is a game of chance, and chances are the gambler will win again. The number of times and amounts of money lost, unfortunately, far outweigh the number of times and amounts of money won. Perpetually playing catch up, problem gamblers accept losing in order to win. Perversely, the very fact of losing further convinces the gambler of the inevitability of winning. She must keep gambling in order for luck to turn around.

The Poor Who Gamble

It is not only those who have won in the past and are now losing who are drawn into compulsive gambling for the money. Those with limited financial resources in the first place are targets for the get-rich-quick lure of gambling—especially, according to research, the state lotteries. The NGISC report revealed how the gambling industry disproportionately affects the poor. The NGISC found that "players with household incomes under $10,000 a year bet nearly three times as much on lotteries as those with incomes over $50,000."[8]

Dr. James Dobson, head of Focus on the Family and one of the NGISC commissioners, expressed his outrage over the impact of gambling on the poor this way: "Gambling is touted as the ticket out of poverty, offering a last chance to riches. As such, it overtly preys on the desperation of the poor by peddling false hope."[9]

This desperation of the poor arises out of an ongoing financial need as opposed to a monetary crisis brought about by gambling behaviors. The poor may not have experienced a big win that ignites the desire to gamble. Instead, false hope alone, perpetuated through advertising and promotional venues, lures the poor into spending their limited financial resources on gambling. The depth of their need is so high, only the promoted financial payoff of gambling is seen as a way out of their dire financial situation.

This get-rich message is further strengthened by the addition of get-rich-quick messages. Not only do many see gambling as a way out of a financial predicament, they see it as an *immediate* way out. Winning the lottery in one enormous win is a dream many of the poor have for escaping the perpetual nature of their poverty. They are willing to spend precious dollars for the dream of waking up wealthy one morning.

This false hope makes an already desperate financial situation even worse. The participants of the NGISC heard testimony from people who had taken their children's milk money in order to gamble or cashed in their welfare checks and spent the money on lottery tickets.[10] The commission found that those living in poverty were some of the most susceptible to the false promise of gambling's rewards and the least cognizant of its true costs.

At the heart of either the gambling poor or the poor who gamble is the desperation to fix their financial state. The gambling poor turn to established habits of wagering in hopes the next bet, the next pot, the next race will provide them with relief from their crushing debt. The poor who gamble turn to the false promises of the gambling promoters, who beguile them with dreams of financial freedom awaiting them with the purchase of the next ticket. Both are deluded about the overwhelming odds against winning. Both are bedazzled by the hope of an all-at-once solution to their poverty. Both are seeking gambling's payoff, failing to recognize the only assured payoff in gambling is off gamblers like themselves.

No Way Out

Though the motivations to begin gambling and the reasons for continuing to gamble may differ, the results of the gambling pattern are the same. Whichever way the problem gambler entered the maze of gambling, once inside, all are trapped as they find themselves deeper and deeper within gambling's environs and subject to its rules.

Those rules can become a source of comfort as the gambling environment becomes a known environment. The entire experience is familiar, and in familiarity there is comfort. The gambler knows what it is like to lose, and she also knows what it is like to win. Other venues for producing income may not be as familiar or comfortable for the gambler. The need to win, coupled with the familiarity of the surroundings and circumstances, produces an overwhelming urge to return again and again to the same gambling situation. Sooner or later, the gambler decides, it will be "my turn to win."

In an attempt to wrest a measure of control from the gambling environment, problem gamblers will look to outside factors. Compulsive gamblers often have elaborate rituals to enhance their luck. They may return to the same set of slots or to the same card dealer or to the same type of gambling venue because it has proved lucky in the past. They may wear certain clothes or carry a good luck charm. They may only gamble at a certain time of the day or only on certain days of the week. None of these behaviors in any way alters the statistical outcome of their gambling, but they are unable to see that. Instead, these rituals are comforting, augmenting the false hope of repeating or enjoying a win.

For the gambling poor and the poor who gamble, the desperation of financial straits distorts the ability to see their situation clearly. The majority of people who gamble are able to view the activity, weigh its risks, and make competent judgments about their level of involvement. For those who fall into the pit of compulsive gambling, need, desire, false hope, or ritual has superseded rational thought. A look at some of the common misconceptions about gambling reveals how thinking gets completely turned around:

- Odds of winning mean nothing because they have won before and "beaten" the odds.
- Losing money is viewed as acceptable in order to turn their luck around and thus win back the money.
- Desperation fuels the false hope that gambling will rescue them from the very situation it has produced.
- Random chance is viewed as luck, which can be manipulated by rituals, outside factors, or simply by their overwhelming desire to win.

The gambling poor and the poor who gamble see gambling as the way out of their financial situation. Rather than evaluate the reason for their situation logically, they choose to concentrate on the false hope of gambling as the solution.

3

LONG WAY TO THE TOP

There he was now. Brian could see Andrew entering the cafeteria, lunch in hand. Only it wasn't Andrew's lunch anymore, it was Brian's. Without saying a word, Andrew walked up to where Brian slouched against the table and set the lunch down.

"Hey, thanks, man," Brian said, reaching for the sack. "Three more weeks to go!" Andrew said nothing in response as he turned and walked out of the lunchroom.

Ham sandwich, bag of chips, and a package of cookies. No pop in it this time, but Brian wasn't going to quibble. He felt a fleeting twinge of guilt at taking Andrew's lunch every day for the past two weeks, but he figured that in a way he'd earned it. Actually, he was doing Andrew a favor, allowing him this unique method to pay off his debt.

Besides, he was teaching him a valuable lesson. Andrew had been so sure of himself. Prided himself in his knowledge of sports, especially football. Always had an opinion about which team was going to win and by how much. Brian felt duty bound to dissuade him of that misguided belief in his own infallibility. Basically, he'd dared Andrew to put his money where his mouth was. Now it was Brian's mouth wrapped around Andrew's sandwich.

Andrew had lost too much money betting on those *Monday Night Football* games. Desperate to make up for his mounting losses, he'd started accepting Brian's offers of "double or nothing." Geometric progression had been Andrew's downfall.

Magnanimous in victory, Brian had come up with the notion of the lunches. Since his mother gave him cash each week to buy lunch, he figured he'd pocket that money and satisfy himself with Andrew's lunch. Funny, he had to admit, it wasn't just the lunch anymore that was satisfying, although Andrew's mom put together a great lunch. Even better to Brian was the ritual of Andrew coming every day into the cafeteria and handing over his lunch. It was like Andrew admitting all over again that Brian had won, that Brian was better. Yes, that was even more satisfying than the money.

MORE THAN THE MONEY

Not all gambling is wagered against an impersonal "house." Not all gambling pits the gambler against the mere odds of winning. Many gambling activities come down to someone named Andrew betting against someone named Brian. Often the chosen field of battle for these contests is sports. While the athletic contest rages on the field, in the arena, or down the court, sideline gamblers wait for an outcome of their own. Those who choose this form of gambling can do so for more than the money. Sometimes the payoff is bragging rights.

On one level, gambling is about luck. A bet is placed and won or lost. If the bet is won, money is gained. If lost, the money is forfeited. Right place, right time—you win. Wrong place, wrong time—you don't. On this level, it's a relatively simple transaction. While gamblers may go through elaborate rituals hoping to enhance their luck, the win comes down to random chance. For some gamblers that simply isn't stimulating enough.

Gambling against individuals, however, can be more complicated. A bet is considered before it is placed. Who is the bet against? What are the terms of the bet? How can the bet be modified to best advantage? How can the person against whom the bet is made be manipulated? What is known about the object of the bet? How much does the person know about what they are betting on? Win or lose, what can be learned about the other person for use in future betting?

For people who gamble against others, it may not be about winning as much as it is about conquering. Winning isn't enough. Someone else needs to lose. Bets are placed with an emphasis on competition, not cash.

SELECTIVE WAGER

This isn't the type of gambler who goes to Las Vegas three times a year and blows a week's salary on the slots. This isn't the type of gambler who sits for hours in front of a video monitor playing poker. Nor is this the type of gambler who stands in line at the grocery store to buy a weekly allotment of lottery tickets. This type of gambler is selective.

Their wagering is selective because they desire to manipulate the odds of winning. They shun casino-style wagering because they understand the overwhelming odds that must be overcome in order to win. Games of chance are much more risky than placing bets on events or situations they understand. This is why sports betting is so compelling to this type of gambler. Each player, each position, every nuance of the game can be tracked, factored, and weighed. Also, in sports betting, a person can wager not only on who wins but by how much.

The most successful of this type of gambler is intelligent. They must be in order to process large amounts of information before making a bet. They are also intuitive, with an ability to assess factors others overlook. Reading people very well, they know who can be bluffed and who cannot. They know how much is just enough to get the other person to take the bet.

This is intricate, intellectual wagering. Previous statistics can be tracked. Existing conditions can be factored. Potential match-ups can be weighed. Bets are placed on the basis of knowledge and intuition rather than the chimera of luck. For this type of gambler, wagering ceases to be a gamble as he relies on intellect to manipulate the situation. In the mind of this gambler, winning results from superior intellect, not random chance. Sure, winning builds up the wallet, but it also builds up the ego.

In individual gambling, when one person wins, the other person loses. There is no large, impersonal house absorbing wins and losses with electronic precision. The wins and losses are personal. While the ego of the winner is inflated, the ego of the loser is deflated. The winner has an advantage over the loser. It is this advantage of power and position that is more alluring than the money.

Top Dog

In our society we are in authority over some people and under the authority of others. This is true for each person, from the highest executive to the lowest worker. While most people can handle being in authority, not everyone is comfortable being under the authority of others. Those who are discontent will choose ways to elevate themselves, and this kind of gambling can be one of those ways. It is a way to establish significance outside of the established channels of society. It is an alternate way to gain advantage, to increase the number of people the gambler has authority over.

This drive to be top dog easily manifests itself through gambling behaviors. At work, this person will initiate betting pools over sporting events, persistently badgering coworkers to participate. At home, this person will engage family members in discussions of a current event, using those discussions to set up a wager based on the outcome of the event. In a social setting, this person will encourage others in the group to bet for recreation or to enhance the social experience.

Whatever the reason, this person is relentless. Any and all situations are fodder for gambling. The wager could be as simple as a quarter a hole in a round of golf. It could be a wager on how soon the taxi will arrive, with the loser paying for the fare. It could be a cup of coffee to the winner of a memory contest over yesterday's box scores while waiting for the elevator. Everyday activities are not fulfilling to this person unless there is some sort of wager associated with them.

For What It's Worth

For this type of gambler, money is not the end-all. It is the constant jockeying for position that he craves. Insecure, this gambler seeks to establish value and position. Because of his insecurity, value and position must continually be fortified through repetition. One bet is never enough. One win does not satisfy because it's not about the money. It's about confirming this gambler's self-image of being intelligent, canny, or shrewd.

A single wager is insufficient to sustain this self-image, so this gambler needs repetition. What is really needed is someone else to bet against. Not everyone is willing to bet, however, especially if he has bet before and lost. In order for the wagering to continue, either another person must be bet against or the gambler must alter the means of payment. If the gambler depletes the pool of potential bettors, there are only two alternatives. One is to manipulate past bettors into gambling again. The other is to entice those who have not gambled in the past to start. In order to maintain the pool of bettors, this gambler allows alternative methods of payment or reduces the amount of the payment. The objective is to continue to bet against another person, which can only be done if that person is willing.

At some point, of course, many people will simply refuse to bet. This will not immediately deter this type of gambler. Not only is this gambler aware of the nuances of the wager, he is also very aware of the characteristics and personalities of the person against whom the bet is made. This gambler will cajole, flatter, embarrass—in short, manipulate—the other person into continuing the betting behavior. The gambler will reduce the amount of the bet or remove money altogether and pursue the bet "just to see who wins." And who loses.

This person is known for gambling. The wagering is constant, interwoven through the gambler's life and relationships. It is a defining aspect of his character. Gambling is how he relates to the world with information and people constantly filtered through gambling. This person is obsessed with gambling though he never steps into a casino or buys a lottery ticket.

Ironically, though able to read others well, this gambler is less able to read himself. The present conviction in his intellectual prowess translates into a false assurance of the successful outcome of any wager. The gambler says, "I *will* win because I *am* smart." Once this thinking takes hold, it is important to the gambler to maintain the illusion since it provides the assurance of both intellect and victory. He is likely to assume that negative events and consequences are not a reflection of his own actions. As he takes less responsibility for poor outcomes, he becomes even less self-aware. It is difficult to break through this barrier and get at the truth. For some, truth only comes when the shambles of lives and relationships are impossible to ignore.

4

LOOKING FOR CONTROL

T. J. couldn't wait to go in to work today. Usually he dreaded the thought of going. To him it meant getting up earlier than he wanted and wearing clothes he disliked. It meant mindless tasks assigned by mindless supervisors. Trading in his valuable time for a too-small paycheck. If he didn't need the money, there's no way he'd go into work, but he always seemed to need the money. His life reminded him of that bumper sticker, "I owe, I owe, so off to work I go." He hated work because it made him feel like a dwarf. But not today.

Today he was a giant. He'd won big. His team had really come through for him the night before. Money was going to be rolling in today, and not from his pathetic hourly wage. Three guys from his division and a gal from the next building over owed him money today. Together his winnings would equal far more than his paycheck this week. Easy money. No FICA deduction, no federal taxes taken out, no workman's comp or medical insurance bleeding him dry. All of it his—in cash.

As he drove past the entrance and made his way to his assigned parking area, T. J. felt that knot starting to form in his stomach. Go here, go there, do this, do that, sign here—last name first, first name next, middle initial. Always in such simple language, like he was an idiot who couldn't follow instructions. It wasn't that he couldn't follow instructions; he was just sick of following *their* instructions. How he'd love to quit and tell them what he really thought about their stupid job.

But he needed the money, so he didn't leave. Maybe, if things kept going his way, he wouldn't need their money so much. It looked like he'd found a way to get money on his own.

MONEY MEANS CONTROL

In many ways this type of gambler is the flip side of the one discussed in the previous chapter. For Brian, it was more about the wager and less about the money; it was more about the win and less about the winnings. For gamblers like T. J., it's all about the money. Money is everything. Through money they have the control they want over their lives. The more money, the more control.

Sporting events provide a popular venue for gamblers who seek control through money. Sports offer a constant source of events to use as a platform for wagering. On any given day, some sporting event is taking place. In addition, the major sports all have special national contests that capture the imagination and the wagering of large portions of the American public, if not the world. The World Series in baseball, the Super Bowl in professional football, the Bowl Championship Series in college football, the NBA Finals in professional basketball, March Madness in college basketball, the Stanley Cup in hockey, the World Cup in soccer—the list goes on and on.

Besides a bewildering array of sporting events to bet on, sports also provide a constant source of enthusiasts against whom to wager. One can usually find somebody who will take up the cause of the other team. It could be a bet placed with a bookie or with the guy at the next desk. With bookies legal in Las Vegas, the distance between a gambler and someone else willing to take her bet is easily bridged by a phone call or modem connection.

Not only are sports ongoing, they involve an aspect of diminished risk for the gambler. Often the more a person learns about a given sport, the more she reduces the risk of losing. Upsets happen all the time, of course, so the risk cannot be completely reduced, but a gambler can often be successful through a thorough investigation of the event upon which the bet is placed. This type of gambler is looking for control in life and deliberately chooses a venue for wagering that she feels she has some control over.

For this type of gambler, the lure is not the sights and sounds of the casino, the hazy dream of winning the lotto, or the satisfaction of being more strategic than someone else. The hook is the control gained through money. People who are drawn to this form of gambling may resent the control they perceive that others have over them. Impatient to be free from that control, they choose wagering as a shortcut to financial prosperity.

Financial prosperity is viewed as financial freedom. Lack of control, the lack of ability to do what they want when they want, is oppressive. Money means freedom to take charge of their lives. Feeling oppressed, they view others as having more than they do. This is not so much a case of keeping up with the Joneses as it is *getting even* with the Joneses. The gambler is fueled by discontent with her own life and jealousy over the lives of others.

In order to make money or earn a salary, most people cede control over their time to an outside force, an employer. That employer controls them during work hours. Not only is their time controlled, the money they earn is also controlled through payroll deductions, taxes, and union or professional dues. This type of gambler chafes under these conditions and resorts to gambling as a source of controllable funds. Removed from the oversight of others, with funds at her complete discretion, she gains satisfaction from feeling in charge. Power and control are the aphrodisiacs seducing the discontent into gambling.

When a casino or a state lottery pays off a winner, there are meticulous rules governing the payment of taxes on those winnings and a record is kept, detailing who has won and how much. In large payouts, taxes are deducted before the winner receives any money. When someone is gambling for control through money, however, the money is often "under the table" and remains hidden from payroll deductions and income taxes. When bookies are used, unless used through legal Las Vegas activities, the gambling is illegal as well as unreported. Gambling under the table leaves more money to the sole control of the gambler.

CHAFING AT THE BIT

For the gambler who wants control, working is a source of frustration, not satisfaction. She feels overlooked at work or feels that the work is beneath her talents and abilities. The job does not capture her imagination or passion; it is merely a means to a paycheck. As a result, she may travel from job to job with extended intervals of unemployment between. If her gambling is successful, she will choose to work less or not at all. If gambling is unsuccessful, she will scale down her lifestyle or take another nonsatisfying job, increasing the amount of resentment.

Coupled with feeling that her work is undercompensated is the feeling that other people's work is overcompensated. Looking around and comparing herself to others, all that is seen is inequity. Rarely does this gambler ever consider the financial rewards of others as gained through perseverance, hard work, and sacrifice. Others make more, others who aren't as smart. Others get more of the breaks in life.

If the key word for this type of gambler is *control,* the key emotion is *frustration.* She is frustrated with her life and how poorly it's going. She is frustrated with other people's lives and how well they are going. Gambling, and the money it promises, provides a way to vent this frustration. Gambling provides a way to even the score.

THE NEW KID ON THE BLOCK

Although sports are a significant wagering platform for this type of gambler, another form of gambling is becoming attractive to those seeking financial control. Through the technology of the Internet, the stock market is becoming the racetrack of the new millennium. Over the World Wide Web, people have an incredible amount of information regarding bond markets, stock offerings, commodities trading, currency exchanges, and other complex financial strategies. The euphoria of "win, place, or show" is replaced by the euphoria of the IPO (initial public offering) of a hot new Internet stock. When people think of gambling on the Internet, they might hesitate to include day-trading. But for the gambler wanting control, betting on the stock market provides the same type of complex, lucrative wager without any of the lingering negative social repercussions of more traditional forms of gambling. (A further discussion of gambling over the Internet can be found in chapter 7.)

THE DOWNWARD SPIRAL

This gambler teeters on a perpetual emotional edge. Euphoria results from winning, providing a temporary relief from the ever-present frustration. When the gambler loses, euphoria turns to despair. Despair turns to anger, as the loss confirms to the gambler that life is somehow always against her. When this storm of rage dissipates, what remains is the hollow feeling of deep depression: "Life is never going to change. The odds will always be against me. Someone else will always get the break; I never will. I will always be underappreciated and overlooked."

This pattern represents a roller-coaster ride of ups and downs, each downward slide plummeting the gambler into deeper bouts of depression. These mood swings of euphoria, despair, and anger alienate those around the gambler, who are dragged along for the ride. Some of those who have a relationship with the gambler will exit the ride quickly and others will be flung out of the relationship when it takes an especially sharp downturn. It is difficult for other people to stay in long-term relationships with the gambler. Friends evaporate. Spouses leave. Families break apart.

This difficulty in relationships extends to employment situations as well. The gambler already resents the control of her job, boss, or coworkers, and this hostility erects a barrier. This barrier hampers an employer's ability to see beyond irresponsible behavior or poor performance to the underlying struggle of the employee. Some who might respond can't see it. Others, who do see it, won't respond. In either case, gambling threatens the very job the gambler resents.

As this spiral digresses, the gambler's erratic emotions degrade her ability to reason. Although the gambler may win at the beginning, the "losing phase" eventually comes. When this happens, her wagering may take on a more desperate form, with a greater reliance on "long shots" to produce large enough payoffs to make up for losses.

The deterioration of reason is also shown through the growing denial that anything is wrong. Erratic emotions produce a warped and false view of reality. The gambler's behavior has crossed into an emotional dimension as she clings desperately to false hope. Logic about gambling or a dispassionate discussion of odds ceases to be persuasive enough to break through this denial.

In any sort of sports betting, odds of winning are factored toward the most logical winner. In other words, if a horse has won three races previously against similar mounts, that record affects what odds are given for winning the current contest. The odds in such a case might be 3:2. In the same field of horses, however, there may be an unproven horse who did not show well at a previous event. The odds of that horse winning might be 7:1. If the second horse wins, the payoff is much greater than the first horse. For a bet of $200 at 3:2 odds, the payoff is $300, a net gain of $100. For that same bet, with 7:1 odds, the payoff would be $1,400, a net gain of $1,200. Of course, the chances of the second horse winning over the first are less, but this gambler may choose the long shot out of desperation.

Logic suggests that a gambler take the 3:2 odds over the 7:1 odds. Logic, however, is subverted in the losing phase. A gambler who previously poured over statistics and information before placing a bet, purchasing a stock, or exercising a commodities option, might now look only for the selection with the highest level of risk and thus the highest payoff.

Before long, the activity the gambler thought would bring increased control over life, now, increasingly, has the control. Obsessed with fulfilling her created fantasy, the gambler loses touch with reality, trading away or giving up things she used to value in order to pursue the fantasy. Against all reason, the gambler continues to place risky bets with control slipping farther and farther away. This is certainly not the payoff for which she had hoped.

THE COMFORT PAYOFF

B etty wanted to hurry, though her knees insisted upon a more deliberate pace. She knew the bus wouldn't leave without her, but truth be known, she was excited to go and didn't want to be late. It had been a month since the last outing, and she was looking forward to the "road trip." After about half a year at this new nursing home, she'd decided to join the group going to the big casino across the state line. It was a five-hour drive, but there were plenty of other seniors to talk to, and she liked sitting up high in the charter bus and watching the world whisk by the tinted window. Lord knows, she saw little enough of the world from the sterile halls of the nursing home. Oh, it was nice and all, but sometimes it felt like slow death. The casino was bright and loud, with lots of people, good food—it was alive. At her age, Betty needed to feel alive.

She also liked people, and not just people her age. This would be her fourth trip to the casino, and even the dealers and servers were beginning to remember her by name. Tipping generously didn't hurt, of course. It was wonderful to have younger people come up, laugh with her, and tease with her. She was so often invisible to other people or treated with distant politeness. The group she traveled with, and those she met while gambling, were becoming like a second family to Betty.

The best part about this family was she didn't have to wait for them to visit her, she could visit them. Every third day of the month, right after her Social Security check came in the mail, the bus showed up like clockwork. Most of her family lived far away, and the son in town never seemed to make it to see her when he promised. Always with a plausible excuse when he called, she knew better. He'd forgotten about her in the rush of his own life and pursuits. She wasn't forgotten though at the casino.

Well, she was ready, if she could only find that hat. Anna down the hall knocked on the door to tell her it was time. Gathering up her purse, Betty checked her wallet to count again how much money she'd brought. She usually managed to spend quite a bit, but she had great credit, and the casino was willing to extend it every time she'd asked. Her son would probably be shocked to know just how much she spent, but she didn't care. If he wasn't interested in the other parts of her life, he had no right to be interested in this. It wasn't his money, anyway, although she often wondered if he thought it was.

Looking back at her room to make sure everything was turned off, she couldn't help but think of the contrast. Her room was dark and lifeless, but she wasn't. In a few moments, knees willing, she'd board that bus and prove it.

MISERY LOVES COMPANY

Legal scholar Erika Gosker says the casino industry tailors marketing strategies toward senior citizens because of the time and the money they have to spend. Targeting this age group, they will pick up seniors like Betty at nursing homes and senior centers, offering free rides and free food. Some casinos even use video cameras to identify those who gamble heavily and target specific age groups. Gosker further writes that older people have a greater risk for problem gambling because of specific circumstances attributed to their age: loneliness, boredom, or the death of a spouse.[1]

An American Association for Retired Persons (AARP) March 2000 article quotes Timothy A. Kelly, executive director of the NGISC, as saying, "Many of the casinos that have sprung up…literally bus people from older persons' homes daily. We heard a lot of stories about elderly parents gambling away the family inheritance."[2] Dr. James Dobson, also a NGISC participant, in his summary statement of the survey, called this practice "one of the most scandalous features of the gambling industry."[3]

Why would people who have lived long enough to learn a lesson or two about life willingly squander what took a lifetime to build?

Loneliness

Loneliness is a crushing weight in the lives of many people, including the elderly. The endless parade of solitary days drains the hope out of many lives. For relief, the lonely will turn to almost anything. This quiet despair is not lost on those who profit from gambling.

Loneliness is, at its base, a loss of connection. Destination gambling provides the lonely a place—a place to go, a place to be, a place to connect. Casinos, card rooms, and bingo parlors are all places where the lonely can make connections. The price for that connection is gambling, and the forgotten, overlooked people of this world are increasingly willing to pay it. It is worth the price to have their relationship and intimacy needs, if not met, at least acknowledged. Financial expenditures can seem a small price to pay for someone to feel noticed.

Camaraderie

The gambling industry takes note of all gamblers. Because of the tendency toward ritual exhibited by gamblers, many tend to be predictable. Not only can the casinos predict where they will play, what they will play, and how much they will gamble, so can other gamblers. This ability to track and predict the actions of other gamblers helps to foster a sense of familiarity within a given gambling group. This accelerated sense of familiarity gives the lonely the sense of connection they are looking for. Add to this the exaggerated attention of paid gambling industry employees, and the effect of gambling on the lonely can be overwhelming.

This phenomenon of a group of different people all coming together and socializing over a common activity is widely known. From the camaraderie of a sports team to the welcoming nods of regulars at a bar, we appreciate being known and knowing others. With casinos, card rooms, and bingo halls popping up in forty-seven different states, there are more places than ever to entice those seeking familiar faces.

Boredom

If loneliness is a quiet despair, boredom can be a gnawing agitation. This is especially true for people who have been active in the past and now find themselves with little to do. The passivity of a lack of stimulation turns into an active torment over time. Quiet is not tranquil, but torture. For some of these people, there is nothing worse than time on their hands. Gambling gives them something to do, something with which to fill up those dead spaces in their day.

When people gamble, things happen. At any moment, the right card could be drawn, the last number could be called, the last coin could be slotted. Gambling activities are just that—active. This constant flow of events guarantees a release from tedium for the bored.

These gamblers are different from the thrill seekers profiled in the first chapter. The thrill seekers gamble to experience the rush of excitement found in the risk of gambling. For the bored, it is not what they are running to but what they are running from that draws them to gamble. The former runs to excitement while the latter runs from boredom. Restless, the bored seek out a way to replace the monotony with activity.

UNFAIR TRADE

Does the gambling experience really keep this type of gambler from experiencing loneliness or boredom? Perhaps for a brief amount of time it does. After the gambling is over, though, the problem reasserts itself. The person who gambles for comfort realizes it is only for that moment. Like Cinderella when the clock struck twelve, the gambler knows that after the last bet is placed, the coach turns into a pumpkin and the gown to rags.

The gambler's answer to this problem of comfort's transitory nature is repetition. It is not by chance the gambling industry targets lonely and bored populations. They know these gamblers return time and time again. These gamblers may not spend an extreme amount of money each time they gamble, but given the frequency of their gambling, over time the net effect is considerable.

The net result of repetition, ironically, is often boredom. The current idiom for this is "Been there—done that." The casino industry responds to this natural tendency by providing an array of gambling and related experiences at destination resorts. Not only are there a variety of gambling choices, there are elaborate entertainment shows, shopping opportunities, and amusement-park attractions added to the mix. The casinos' answer for boredom with gambling is not to leave permanently but to "take a break" from gambling, so the gambler is refreshed and ready to gamble again.

The more the gambler returns to gambling, the more ingrained the pattern will be. The more ingrained the pattern, the quicker it is sought whenever comfort is needed. Gamblers seeking comfort from gambling tend to use gambling as a sort of "white noise," numbing discomfort. Pain, boredom, and loneliness all cause discomfort that can be momentarily blocked by gambling behaviors. Gambling doesn't make the pain go away, but it provides a respite. Eventually the gambling may no longer provide active comfort but only numb the pain. The gambler then accepts momentary cessation of the pain in place of comfort.

This pattern robs us of the vitality of life. Joy is downgraded to lack of feeling. Excitement is traded for predictability. Intimacy is bartered for acquaintance. Cheapened, the gambler begins to feel even less significant than before. Rather than providing a sense of connection, gambling loosens connections as its false promises replace relationships with others and with ourselves.

6

THE NEXT GENERATION

B eads of condensation traced a slow path down the side of the glass. Numb, Casey could do nothing more than observe their gradual fall from grace. Even the beer inside meant nothing at the moment. Gone, all gone, every bit of his tuition money. It was now tucked inside Will's coat pocket.

Will had allowed him to keep racking up his gambling tab, deferring each loss. At first, Casey thought Will was doing him a favor, helping out a buddy in the same philosophy class. Now he knew Will was merely giving him enough room, enough rope, to hang himself. Thirteen hundred dollars worth of rope. He'd paid it off tonight with his tuition money. The beer was a consolation prize.

Casey still had his work-study job, of course, but he didn't work that many hours. The tuition money was due to the school by the end of next week, and now he didn't have it. Suddenly impatient, Casey gathered up the glass in his hand, crushing the condensation and putting the watery droplets out of their misery. Tipping back the glass, he attempted to drown his own.

Options, what were his options, he wondered, as he wiped a wet hand against his pant leg. He could try to get a loan from somebody. He could tell his parents an emergency had come up and he'd had to use the money for that. He could tell his parents the truth and ask for more tuition money. None of these options seemed likely to succeed.

Nobody he knew had that kind of money to loan him. All of his friends were scraping by like he was. And he still owed three of them anywhere between twenty to fifty bucks. They'd already loaned him all they were going to.

His parents would want to know just what the emergency was. After all, it was their money he'd spent. They'd want to know why he'd waited until after it was spent to come to them. They were already suspicious, in a general way, of what was happening at school. His mom had commented, when he'd been home a few weeks earlier, that he seemed "distracted."

If he told them the truth, he'd have to...well, tell them the truth. It'd be a nightmare. His dad would be angry and disappointed. His mom wouldn't say anything at first, just look devastated. He couldn't blame them, really—that was how he felt too.

There was another option, though, now that he thought about it. Gambling had gotten him into this mess, maybe it wasn't too late to get him out of it. After all, a week and a half was a long time. The playoffs were starting, and there'd be plenty of bets flying around. All he needed was some seed money to get started. He'd pulled himself out of a few tough spots before. He remembered the time in high school he'd bet the money his dad had given him for his letterman's jacket. That had been a close call, but he'd managed to win it all back and then some. The jacket was still hanging in his closet at home.

Yeah, all he needed was some cash. Resolved, he downed the dregs of the beer and stood up to leave. As he started weaving his way down the aisle to the exit, Casey noticed four dollar bills. A tip someone had left for the waitress, splayed like a hand of cards on the edge of an upcoming tabletop. It was a sign. With barely a hesitation, Casey gathered them up in his hand and into his pocket as he headed out the door.

STARTING EARLY

Casey is just one member of the first generation to have grown up in a culture where gambling is widespread and socially acceptable. Throughout his early years and adolescence, gambling has been a part of his culture. Grocery and convenience stores sell lottery tickets. Horse tracks and dog tracks are visible from the freeway. Card rooms advertise on the same signs as dry cleaners and vacuum-cleaner repair shops. Wagering on sporting events and card games is defined as family fun. Dotcoms leave spammed e-mail messages in electronic mailboxes touting the latest gambling conduit. Gambling is all around him, and Casey has joined in. Casey is not alone.

A recent study in Washington State among adolescents found that 78 percent of those surveyed reported having placed at least one bet at some time, 65 percent said they had gambled in the past year, and 8 percent bet on one or more types of gambling at least once a week or more often.[1] Wagering with family or friends on card games, dice games, and board games was popular with adolescents, as well as gambling on games of skill and sports.[2] At school, at home, and with friends, young people are incorporating gambling behaviors into their leisure activities. Gambling is influencing, infiltrating, and enhancing the games of youth.

When the National Research Institute (NRI) looked at reports on the number of adolescents who have gambled at some point in their lives, they found estimates ranging from 39 percent to 92 percent. The median percentage was 85. When the NRI looked at the percentage of adolescents who had gambled during the previous year, the range was from 52 percent to 89 percent, with a median percentage of 73.3. These figures represent a staggering number of children engaging in underage gambling activity.

A question has been raised over whether children participate in gambling by chance or by design of the gambling industry. In his summary statement to the NGISC, Dr. James Dobson sounded a cry of alarm when he said, "some of the most troubling evidence received by the Commission concerned the manner in which the gambling industry and its allies in government work together to cultivate betting habits in the next generation."[4] Dobson cited concerns about children having access to video poker machines in convenience stores, pizza parlors, and bowling alleys. He brought attention to the way in which casinos, through amusement rides and arcades, provide children with virtual copies of their adult gambling experiences. He asked, "What kind of message are we sending to our children?" after commenting on the evidence of overwhelming access by minors to state-promoted lotteries.[5]

What kind of message indeed?

McLOTTO

In the midst of his work on the NGISC, Dr. Dobson was confronted in his home state of Colorado by a gambling-related promotion by McDonald's. Called "McLotto Meals," this promotional campaign in 1998 by Colorado McDonald's restaurants offered coupons for lottery tickets with the purchase of certain meals. Dr. Dobson's organization, Focus on the Family, urged McDonald's to withdraw the lottery promotion. In a letter to the chairman and CEO of McDonald's, Dr. Dobson stated, "I find it most disturbing that a respected corporation which appeals to children promotes gambling as an acceptable and harmless activity."[6] McLotto may have been crafted for adults only, but Dr. Dobson, through his work on the NGISC, knew differently. Because of McDonald's intentional tie-in with children, the McLotto campaign was sure to influence the restaurants' youngest customers.

The commissioners of the NGISC were very concerned about these young customers. They received firsthand information on the failure of the gambling industry to keep children away from gambling. They also learned that 27 percent of fifteen- to eighteen-year-olds in Minnesota had purchased lottery tickets. In Louisiana, it was 32 percent; in Texas, it was 34 percent; and in Connecticut, it was 35 percent. In Massachusetts, where state lottery tickets are available through self-service vending machines, the state attorney general's office found that minors as young as nine years old were able to purchase lottery tickets in 80 percent of their attempts.[7] Across the country, adults-only gambling has been proven to be an illusion.

While the lottery may be a harmless recreation for the majority of adults, it can prove far from harmless for children. For many young people, an experience with a lottery provides a gateway to other types of gambling and addictive behaviors. This concern was voiced in the executive summary of the Washington State study mentioned previously: "There is concern that lottery gambling may be an experience that encourages young people to engage in other, less broadly sanctioned types of gambling as well as in other risk-taking behaviors, such as illicit drug use. A significant increase in lottery play by age was identified among Washington State adolescents. While 6 percent of thirteen-year-olds in the Washington State sample have purchased lottery tickets in the past year, 21 percent of the seventeen-year-olds have done so. The increase in lottery play is correlated with increased participation in other types of gambling and in use of alcohol, tobacco and marijuana."[8]

In his news release regarding the Colorado McLotto promotion, Dr. Dobson acknowledged that the company was "likely oblivious" to the realities surrounding young people, the lottery, and gambling behaviors. As gambling has increased across the country, in adults and in children, these realities are now noticed.

Recent research points to the escalating nature of youthful gambling. Information by the National Council on Problem Gambling illustrates this escalation: While 42 percent of fourteen-year-olds gamble, the number jumps to 49 percent for fifteen-year-olds, 63 percent for sixteen-year-olds, 71 percent for seventeen-year olds, 76 percent for eighteen-year-olds, and by nineteen years of age, 88 percent say they have gambled.[9]

The evidence is overwhelming that young people are imitating adult behavior by gambling. The evidence is also compelling that once they begin to gamble, the young have higher incidences of problem and at-risk gambling behaviors. A Harvard Medical School Center for Addiction Studies analysis of youth gambling in North America found problem gambling among youths ranged from 9.9 percent to 14.2 percent. Those who were already showing signs of what the report termed "compulsive gambling behaviors" increased that total by a range of 4.4 percent to 7.4 percent.[10] In the Washington State study, the number for problem and at-risk adolescent gamblers was placed at 8.4 percent. And while adolescents represented approximately 7 percent of the total population of the state, they accounted for between 12 percent and 18 percent of those "experiencing severe difficulties related to their gambling."[11]

These cold statistics lead us to ask personal questions: Why are teens so drawn to gambling? In what ways do we inadvertently foster destructive behavior?

Sportsmanship

One of the favorite ways for young people to gamble is over sporting events. Influenced by athletic superstars, young people seek to participate in sporting events in a variety of ways. Many play these sports on a school or intramural level. Even more watch sporting events, rooting for favorite teams and following favorite stars. Some bet on these events. The NGISC executive summary warned: "There is growing concern regarding increasing levels of sports wagering by adolescents in high school and by young adults on college campuses. A 1996 study sponsored by the National Collegiate Athletic Association found that of the over 2,000 student athletes surveyed in Division I basketball and football programs, 25.5 percent admitted betting on college sports events while in school."[12]

Sports betting by the young combines hero worship with athletic competition with the lure of winning. This combination is causing problems for more and more young people at home and at school.

Follow the Leader

Children live in a world of the possible. Their view of life is buoyed by an ever-changing landscape of new discoveries, new abilities, and expanding vistas. Children believe. They may have always believed in their parents, in their teachers, in God, and in their friends. Now they believe in gambling. And why shouldn't they when the adults around them do? Why shouldn't they when television touts gambling as a way out of life's problems? Why shouldn't they when a significant number of the adults around them answer a resounding "I do!" when asked, "Who wants to be a millionaire?"

While a child's view of possibilities is expansive, their understanding of consequences is limited. Some consequences manifest only after the passage of time. Children haven't been around long enough for those consequences to surface. Many simply have not yet experienced the inevitable downside of engaging in risky behaviors. Unaware of its negative undertow, young people dive into gambling for many of the same reasons adults do: thrill, affirmation, money, power, and control.

Without the maturity to recognize the danger and without the knowledge to extricate themselves from that danger, young people are at heightened risk for developing severe problems. According to information from the American Academy of Pediatrics, teen gambling is an indicator of participation in other risky behaviors. "Overall, teens who gambled in the past year doubled their illegal drug use (15 percent) vs. teens who had not gambled (8 percent). Illegal drug use was nearly doubled again (28 percent) by students who reported having problems related to gambling."[13] Teens who gambled were twice as likely to have been in a fight or have carried a weapon in the previous month. Gambling was a common denominator in the likelihood of engaging in other risky behaviors. The more likely teens were to have gambled, the more likely they were to have experienced problems because of it.[14]

As gambling has multiplied dramatically at the state and local levels, governments are scrambling to cope with the increase in the number of their citizens experiencing gambling problems. Unfortunately, those citizens run the gamut of their age populations, from the old to the young, from the seasoned to those starting out, from the most venerable to the most vulnerable.

Section 1 Follow-Up

You've met the gamblers. Remember, though, that people rarely fall into neat categories. Each gambler will probably have traits from several of these profiles. But the reasons for gambling will remain overwhelmingly consistent. I have found that human needs are remarkably few, but the ways in which we go about meeting those needs are amazingly diverse. For many, gambling has become a way to meet their needs.

You've met the gamblers, but who are you? Are you someone who is concerned about how much you enjoy gambling? Are you someone who has a friend or loved one who gambles far too much? Are you that friend or loved one?

If you are concerned about your own gambling, please go through this follow-up section as honestly as you are able. If you felt called to pick up and read this book, honor that call by working with it. Try not to shortchange yourself by only reading or doing those parts that seem comfortable or easy. This self-evaluation is between you and God. No one else needs to be involved unless you choose.

If your concern regarding gambling is for someone else, first go through the follow-up yourself. You may discover you are using ways to meet your needs that are as compelling for you as gambling is for the person you are concerned about. Recognizing this in yourself will help you to understand the gambler better and allow you to have more compassion for their plight. God reminds us in Romans 3:10 that no one is righteous. The gambler doesn't need your judgment. The gambler does need your compassion, love, and understanding.

Then go back and consider the answers to this section as it relates to the person you are concerned about. Carefully evaluate the basis of and evidence for your concern about his or her gambling. This will help you if you feel it necessary to confront your friend about his or her behaviors.

Whether you are a gambler or concerned about someone gambling, ask God for insight and wisdom as you go through this follow-up. Use another sheet of paper to fully develop your answers. Be as honest as you can, with yourself and with God, and he will reward you. Pray and listen for him to speak to you.

Follow-Up

1. Make a list of the things you need in your life.
2. What are some positive ways you are meeting those needs?
3. What are some negative ways you are meeting those needs?
4. Look at the list you've made. Rank your answers for each need in order of importance to you. What do your priorities tell you about how you are meeting your needs?
5. Often when doing evaluations of this kind, we want to put down the "right answers," even if no one else is going to see what we've written. Did you feel that way about the question above? Did you put something down because you thought it was the right answer? Did you avoid putting something down because it makes you look bad? If so, why? What did you put down instead? Why was it difficult to be honest with yourself?
6. If you are a gambler, what needs does your gambling meet? (If you are not the gambler, look at your own life and choose an area where you are meeting a need in an inappropriate way. Put that in the place of gambling in this question.) Are there any other areas in your life where this need is being met? If so, rank those areas according to desire. In other words, if you are filling the need for thrill through gambling and two other areas of your life, which area is most important to you? Which area for meeting that need would you most easily give up and why? Which would you be least likely to give up and why?
7. How has doing this evaluation made you feel? Are you experiencing a feeling of freedom to be able to acknowledge some truths in your life? Are you angry about any of the questions? Are you

frustrated at the time needed to evaluate this section? Whatever
you are feeling, take a moment and explore why you are feeling
this way and what those feelings reveal.

8. Take time to open your heart and your mind to God through
prayer. Ask him to invade your thoughts with his truth. Ask him
to calm any restless feelings you experienced through doing this
follow-up. Thank him for the insights you've gained so far and
ask him to prepare your heart for the next section in the book.

SECTION 2

WHEN CULTURE RAISES
THE STAKES

Gambling, with its high intensity risk-and-reward system, has always been a part of the human experience. Gambling is not a phenomenon unique to our time nor is it a uniquely American phenomenon. The siren song of winning has been heard by many cultures over the span of time.

What is unique about the current gambling situation is the speed at which it has gone from an undercurrent in American society to a high-profile, socially recognized activity. In the past twenty years the culture in this country has taken a dramatic shift in favor of gambling in general and governmentally sanctioned gambling in particular. What was illegal is now state-sanctioned. What was back alley is now Main Street. What was accessible to a few is now available to most. This shift has not arisen because of any grand conspiracy to entrap Americans into a gambling lifestyle. Instead, the change has been occurring in small doses along a vast array of individual venues since the 1970s.

Perhaps the introduction to the NGISC report says it best: "There was no single, overarching national decision to turn the United States into a world leader in gambling. Rather, games of chance spread across the map as a result of a series of limited, incremental decisions made by individuals, communities, states, and businesses."[1] These "games of chance" have popped up all across our national landscape and changed the culture we live in.

We now live in a culture encouraging an activity that destroys a percentage of the lives it touches. We live in a culture that looks the other way when young people are sucked into adult addictions. We live in a culture that touts the freedom of the strong while tolerating the destruction of the weak. We live in a culture that willingly accepts the revenues of gambling as hush money.

The previous section took a look at the gamblers. We found they are our family members, neighbors, and coworkers. They are people who sit next to us in church pews on Sunday morning. They are often us. Christians who gamble mirror the culture, a culture increasingly tolerant of gambling behaviors and increasingly dependent on gambling revenues. Christians who are trapped in pathological gambling behaviors cannot look to the culture to save them. The culture has caved.

BRIGHT NIGHTS, DARK DAYS

The hotel room was dark except for an annoying sliver of sunlight coming in through the crack in the curtains and waking Jeremy. He'd been aware of it for a while now, though trying to ignore it. His parents and sister were still sleeping, so he got dressed as quietly as possible for a twelve-year-old.

Slipping the hotel key card into his pocket, Jeremy made his way to the elevator and rode down to the lobby and the free continental breakfast. A few older people and another family were just leaving when he arrived. He wasn't really hungry, so he grabbed a donut and a carton of orange juice and headed toward the front of the hotel. He couldn't believe there were people at the casino floor this early in the morning.

Harsh sunlight and the heat of the morning blasted him as he walked outside. When they'd arrived from the airport last night, the air had been cool, the lights dazzling, the sounds exciting, and the smells mouth-watering. This morning the air was hot, the lights were faint in the intensity of the sun, and the only sounds and smells came from the Dumpster around the corner being emptied. This didn't make eating his breakfast any easier.

A bored valet in his early twenties leaned against the side of the building, taking a break and having a smoke. The valet nodded to him as Jeremy ducked under the eaves of the building, out of the sun, to finish his orange juice.

"Doesn't look the same in the morning, does it?" the valet asked, dangling the cigarette from his fingers. Jeremy looked out over the roadway and nodded. He noticed a line of people walking single file along the road, kicking up small clouds of dust in the scrubby, sandy soil.

"What are they doing?" Jeremy asked.

"They're locals," the valet said, finishing off his cigarette, "not tourists walkin' from casino to casino." None of them looked up, eyes averted from the morning sun. Jeremy could see they appeared old, sort of worn-out. When he looked away, the valet had gone, leaving just the butt of his cigarette crushed into the pavement.

Suddenly feeling awkward and a little strange, Jeremy headed back for the hotel and casino. It was a lot nicer inside.

Close to Home

This culture embraces choices. It heralds freedom and individual rights. These values have translated into an acceptance of a growing number of gambling options—options that ironically rob people of their financial and relational freedom. Cultural awareness of the consequences of gambling is slow in coming. Not only is there an explosion in the places people can gamble, there is an explosion in the ways people can gamble. Let's look at a few of the ways government and culture are bringing gambling to our homes and families.

Casino Gambling

It used to be that casino-style gambling existed in only two places: Nevada and Atlantic City. If you wanted a casino-style gambling experience, you needed to travel to either of these two places. They were "destinations." Across the United States, apart from Nevada and Las Vegas, there are now approximately 260 casinos on Indian reservations. Riverboat gambling, either on the water or at a dockside, accounts for almost 100 additional opportunities for casino-style gambling.[1] You can still go to Nevada or Atlantic City to find a casino, but you can also drive a few miles down the nearest interstate.

Americans are traveling to these destinations and spending their leisure dollars. According to the executive summary of the NGISC, "more than $1 in $10 ($50.9 billion) was spent on gambling, not including monies spent by gamblers on hotels, food, transportation and other expenses...accounting for 30.1 billion" in revenues in 1997, more than one-third of all "destination leisure (e.g. spectator sports, cruise ships, theme parks, concerts)" revenue.[2] A recent program on the Discovery Channel stated that more people had visited a casino than had gone to a Major League Baseball stadium to see a game. Baseball used to be called "America's game." A case could be made that America's "game" is now gambling.

Family Friendly

Casinos have always attracted gamblers with a wide variety of gambling experiences, from poker to blackjack, from slots to solitaire, from track racing to sports betting. Since children are legally prohibited from the gambling area, most people used to leave their children at home when they went to gamble at destination locations. Children were bored and distracted parents from gambling. There was nothing to do if you didn't gamble—the casino industry wanted to ensure people would stay on the casino floor. Casinos were not known as being family friendly.

That strategy has changed. Casinos in Las Vegas and Atlantic City now feature "family style" entertainment. Advertisements and casino services have been crafted to lure families to these destinations. Hotels have merged amusement-style rides and visuals with their gambling activities. Mom and Dad are now encouraged to bring the kids. Casinos provide a vacation experience, of which gambling is only a component.

While Dad's playing poker and Mom's at the slots, the kids can try their skill at arcade and video games. There's plenty for them to do until they get old enough to gamble. The casinos are willing to wait and accommodate.

STATE LOTTERIES

Other aspects of the gambling industry have changed as well. According to the NGISC report, in 1973 seven states had lotteries, with sales totaling $2 billion. Twenty-four years later, state lotteries operated "in more than five times as many states" and brought in $34 billion in sales.[3] Lotteries now account for the second largest segment of gambling revenues, after casino gambling.[4] In lotteries, state governments have discovered a large pool of money without the necessity of increased taxation. This lure has proven to be overwhelming in all but three states: Hawaii, Utah, and Tennessee.

Just as the lure of revenue has proven overwhelming to the states, the lure of winning has proven overwhelming to their citizens. If the popularity of state lotteries is in doubt, just observe the long line of customers weaving in and out of grocery store aisles whenever a large jackpot is on the line. Lottery outlets are literally on every corner, with splashy signs and clever slogans, extolling the joys of instant wealth. All of this is courtesy of state and local governments, which use sophisticated marketing strategies to entice their citizens to spend money.

State lotteries combine impressive forces: the lure of winning and the distribution and marketing capabilities of government. Advertising for lotteries pushes the dream of winning millions as a way to either stick it to a lousy boss, get out of a dead-end situation, solve financial difficulties, or release your true potential. For the cost of a dollar—or two or five or twenty—the lottery purchaser buys a chance to dream "what if?" And it's not just winning that is touted. Some ads for lotteries pitch the idea that playing the lottery spices up a ho-hum day. Just buying the ticket is good for you, we're told, even if you don't win a dime.

These dreams are promoted as harmless recreation by the states. Hawked as harmless, fun, and exciting, many states promote lottery sales as an enlightened social contribution. When states first placed lottery proposals before their voters, many used the hook of education to overcome voter anxieties over the negative impacts of gambling in their towns and neighborhoods. Lottery promoters promised that a portion of the revenue would be targeted to educational budgets. Voters approved the lotteries, believing schools would benefit from this "tax-free" financing and lottery money would be used to augment strained education budgets.

True to their promises, many states did earmark money from lotteries to education budgets. However, "several states experienced reductions in actual general funding for programs for which lottery revenue was earmarked."[5] In other words, once state legislatures knew there was lottery money being funneled to the schools, some reduced the size of the state general funding devoted to education, diverting those dollars to other uses. The schools ended up with no more money than before; it just came from a different source.

Demand for lottery sales increases disproportionately in economically depressed areas. According to research for the NGISC, Dr. Phillip Cook and his colleague Dr. Charles Clotfelter "found that lottery players with incomes below $10,000 spend more than any other income group, an estimated $597 per year. Further, high school dropouts spend four times as much as college graduates. Blacks spend five times as much as whites. In addition, the lotteries rely on a small group of heavy players who are disproportionately poor, black, and have failed to complete a high school education."[6]

PARI-MUTUEL BETTING

As other gambling venues grow in popularity, the percentage of total gambling revenues from pari-mutuel betting (betting on races and dividing winnings based on the individual wagers) is sharply declining. The exception to this trend is horse racing. With over 150 racetracks spread over forty-three states, horse racing has remained the most successful form of pari-mutuel wagering. The throaty sound of "And they're off!" produces annual gross revenues of $3.25 billion.

As with casinos, racetracks are "destinations." With the advent of technology, however, more and more people can participate in pari-mutuel betting without ever setting foot at the track. Television and video carry live feed to wagering centers and bookmakers in Las Vegas. Internet technology sends that same live feed directly into the homes of gamblers, offering instant access to races from tracks all over the world. According to the NGISC, eight states currently allow betting on horse racing from home.[7] It remains to be seen how pari-mutuel gambling will be affected as gambling venues vie against each other for customers.

SPORTING EVENTS

As discussed in previous chapters, sports betting represents an enormous outlet for gambling within our culture. Nevada might be the only state where bookmaking on sporting events is legal, but the sheer volume of the informal, illegal type of this betting makes its presence felt all across the country. People may decry the easy accessibility of drugs and weapons in this country, but how many express outrage over the availability of gambling on a sporting event?

As the culture-at-large becomes more comfortable with gambling, instances of casual gambling bubble to the surface. The NGISC noted an increase in office-pool gambling, now out in the open, though still illegal.[8] How long this type of gambling will remain illegal remains to be seen, given its widespread acceptance among Americans. Its legal status may be rendered irrelevant, for when was the last time a newspaper banner heralded the arrest of workers in an office pool?

CONVENIENCE GAMBLING

This form of gambling is also known as "retail gambling." It refers to "legal, stand-alone slot machines; video poker; video keno; and other EGDs (electronic gambling devices) that have proliferated in bars, truck stops, convenience stores, and a variety of other locations across several states."[9] According to research done by the NGISC, these devices can be run by private companies, such as in states like Louisiana or Montana, or they can be run by the state lottery, such as in states like Oregon and California. Perhaps no state has embraced this form of gambling more than South Carolina, where thirty-four thousand licensed video poker machines operate at seventy-five hundred locations.[10]

It is not by chance these devices are placed in convenience stores. They are meant to be convenient to find and use. Like candy bars stacked strategically near checkout counters, electronic gambling devices are placed to take advantage of impulse. Young people easily confuse these machines with the electronic video games in the same part of the store. They look the same and sound the same, but the payout is real. Now a quick run to the market to pick up milk and bread for tomorrow morning can mean making a choice about gambling away the leftover change.

TRIBAL GAMBLING

In 1987 the U.S. Supreme Court ruled that states had a limited ability to regulate commercial gambling on Indian reservations. To better define what that limited ability meant, in 1988 Congress passed the Indian Gambling Regulatory Act (IGRA). The IGRA establishes the line between states' rights and tribal rights, providing the regulatory framework for casino gambling on reservations. Revenues from tribal gambling that year totaled $212 million. Ten years later over 260 casinos were on tribal lands in thirty-one states, and revenues had multiplied to $6.7 billion.[11]

Perhaps no other factor has opened the floodgates of gambling in this country more than that Supreme Court decision. By acknowledging the sovereignty of tribes to permit gambling on their lands, the Court handed an economically disadvantaged people the means to generate revenue apart from the federal and state government. Casinos have been going up ever since as tribes rush to cash in.

This infusion of cash has provided many tribes with additional funds, but it has not always produced the anticipated results. Unemployment among Native Americans remains about 50 percent, while the overwhelming majority of tribal casino workers are not Native Americans.[12] Tribes, even those with gambling establishments, still receive federal assistance.

Far from the panacea for most tribes, casinos on tribal lands have not produced the anticipated bounty. What they have produced is an ever increasing opportunity for Native Americans and others to spend time and money on games of chance.

INTERNET GAMBLING

State gambling commissions regulate casino gambling, lotteries, parimutuel racetracks, and EGDs. The IGRA regulates tribal gambling. The newcomer on the gambling block, the Internet, is not regulated. When compared to the billions of dollars generated in other types of gambling venues, Internet gambling appears to be in its infancy. But if it is an infant, it is growing rapidly. In 1997 Internet gambling grossed about $300 million—a relatively small amount. In 1998 that figure more than doubled to around $651 million. Some estimate that Internet gambling will exceed $2 billion by 2001.[13]

Because of the amazing accessibility the Internet provides, gambling is now available through a modem and a computer screen. Just produce a credit card number, and you'll find sites available. "Technology is revolutionizing the gambling industry as we know it. As the Internet continues to grow, so too does the popularity of online wagering. Seemingly overnight, all forms of gambling have become accessible to every home and every individual twenty-four hours a day. But how prepared is the nation for this kind of evolution within the gambling industry?"[14] The NGISC answered its own question by recommending a moratorium on government approval of further Internet gambling and cutting off the availability of money by prohibiting wire transfers to known Internet gambling sites.[15]

The NGISC report cited concern over the unregulated nature of the Internet and the accessibility American gamblers had to overseas sites.[16] Noting that the governments of Antigua and Australia had recently entered the field of Internet gambling, Tom W. Bell of the Cato Institute spoke to the NGISC of the futility of prohibiting Internet gambling: "The Internet offers an instant detour around merely domestic prohibitions. Principles of national sovereignty will prevent the U.S. from forcing other countries to enforce a ban on Internet gambling, and it takes only one safe harbor abroad to ensure that U.S. citizens can gamble over the Internet."[17]

When the glitzy world of gambling is married to the fast-paced, visual world of the Internet, the pull to gamble is compelling. Visitors on some Internet sites can go on tours of virtual casinos, complete with realistic graphics and music. Other sites offer a lottery or bingo experience. And it doesn't stop there. The Internet boasts about 110 sports-related gambling sites, providing online tournaments that are particularly appealing to young gamblers.[18]

The NGISC study cites three at-risk populations especially susceptible to Internet gambling: young people, pathological gamblers, and criminals. All of these populations find the Internet has advantages that are not available through other forms of gambling. Through the anonymity of the Internet, underage gamblers have access to gambling by merely entering a credit card number without scrutiny. The accessibility of the Internet provides pathological gamblers with their gambling "fix" twenty-four hours a day, seven days a week—online, anytime. Computer hackers find the Internet to be a lucrative feeding ground for money and financial information. Often this criminal element already exists within gambling circles. The merging of the two venues provides the clever criminal with multiple opportunities for ill-gotten gain— especially because he can be in one place, out of U.S. jurisdiction, and still have access to gamblers from all over the world.

As a technology, the Internet is changing the way this culture works. The pace of that change is staggering; however, the implications of that change are sometimes slower to be noticed. The NGISC heard from Dr. Howard J. Shaffer, director of addiction studies at Harvard. Dr. Shaffer compared gambling to an addictive drug, and he suggested that the Internet is a new way to deliver that drug: "As smoking crack cocaine changed the cocaine experience, I think electronics is going to change the way gambling is experienced."[19]

The Internet has already proven to be highly effective in providing other types of addictive activities, such as pornography and video games. Its immediacy, anonymity, and accessibility make it an ideal conduit for addictive behaviors. This is particularly troubling when the segment of the population that is most comfortable with the Internet is young people—the same population that is showing an increased susceptibility to problem and pathological gambling.

Something for Everyone

The amount of gambling choices today is mind-boggling. Gambling is everywhere and therefore the choice to gamble or not to gamble is constant. There is no longer the luxury of "out of sight, out of mind." Just as a person can be a drink away from becoming an alcoholic, today a person can be a bet away from becoming an addicted gambler.

In the case of gambling, specifically casino gambling, familiarity doesn't breed contempt, it breeds more problem gamblers. In fact, it is believed that gambling industry employees are more likely to be addicted to gambling than the general population. Dr. Robert Hunter, a specialist in pathological gambling treatment, has estimated that 15 percent of gambling industry employees have a gambling problem.[20] Those who are around gambling the most appear to have more problems with it. Even so, culture has made the choice to expose greater numbers of the population to gambling opportunities. The consequences of gambling may need to become even more glaring, more obvious, for society to take serious notice. In the meantime, some lives will be ruined and others will be placed at severe risk.

JUST A LITTLE WAGER

K evin! I've got the board set up!" Mark yelled to his brother from the den. He looked down at the table covered with the game board, dice, and tokens, all neat and organized. Anxious to get started, he rearranged the pieces, glancing over his shoulder to the doorway, waiting on Kevin. Part of him was still in shock that his older brother had agreed to play with him. Most of the time, these days, Kevin always seemed to be "too busy."

He wasn't too busy tonight for some reason. After a minute, Kevin came into the den, hands in his pocket, pulling out a wad of bills.

"Hey, Mark, how about we liven this game up and play for money?" he asked as he shoved the bills back into his pocket.

"Real money? You sure that's okay with Mom?"

"Sure, it won't be for much. How about a quarter in the pot every time somebody rolls doubles. At the end of the game, whoever wins the game gets the pot. Okay?" He was busy dumping his change onto the table in front of his chair.

Mark thought about it a minute. He didn't care about the money much, but he had a feeling Kevin wouldn't be so eager to play with him if his answer was no. "Yeah, okay," he said and went to his room to search through his change.

Kevin sat back in the chair. If he was lucky, he could extend the game and pile a few more quarters in the pot. He usually beat Mark whenever they played this game, and it had become boring. Not tonight.

Providing an Entryway

People have always placed bets with each other. They have always played games and competed against each other for a favorable outcome. In and of themselves, games like cards, dice, board games, video games, and sports contests are not harmful. They provide fun and enjoyment when played with family and friends. They can also provide an entryway for people, especially young people, to experience the pull of gambling.

These entry activities are especially troubling because of the research that indicates young people experience problem or at-risk gambling behaviors at twice the rate of adults. In other words, this next generation of adult gamblers will come into their adulthood already twice as likely as the generation before them to have problems with gambling. It is important to be aware of the ways gambling is allowed into our homes, families, and children's lives.

The Entryway of the Family

Most people don't start out deciding they are going to become obsessed with gambling. Instead, gambling is presented to them within the context of their lives. It is presented as enhancing everyday activities, providing excitement and a competitive experience.

According to the findings of the Washington State survey on gambling, young people are most likely to start gambling "on card, dice or board games with friends or family, games of personal skill and sports."[1] Many children, beginning at an early age, see their parents engage in game playing with other adults. From the time they are eye level to the kitchen table or the card table set up in the living room, children are exposed to pinochle, poker, bridge, dominoes, mah-jongg, Scrabble, and

Trivial Pursuit. They see their parents laughing and having fun while playing these games and betting on the outcome. If the children behave well, they are even allowed to handle the money, counting the winnings or carefully putting the coins in piles.

Playing for money is viewed as an adult activity. Children understand the fun of simply playing a game. The addition of money, enhancing the excitement of the game, is understood to be something to look forward to as they grow older.

Children do grow older, and when they begin to gamble, it is with family and friends. Backyards and schoolyards become makeshift gambling halls, complete with well-worn decks of cards and pairs of dice. The stakes are usually small, but the winner and loser feel the same thrill and disappointment no matter how much is in the pot. These experiences are low-key ways for youngsters to get to know how it feels to gamble, to win, to lose. Their opponents are known to them. This type of gambling feels safe and familiar. It provides a comfortable platform for trying other forms of gambling or wagering larger amounts of money.

The Entryway of Sports

As noted earlier, sporting events are perfect venues for gambling activities. There are sporting events for every interest, and the competitive nature of the event lends itself well to wagering. A teenager doesn't need to go far to find this type of gambling. Usually it's down the block or in the next room.

Friends and family aren't wagering to entrap the teen into gambling behaviors, they're just making a friendly bet. But this betting can quickly become unfriendly if the teen develops a pattern of escalating wagering. The research is clear that the wagering done on sports between family members and friends is an entry activity, used by young people to "get their feet wet" in gambling experiences.

The Entryway of Collectibles

They used to come inside the wrapper of bubble-gum packages, the smell conjuring up images of dusty, pink chews. They used to have pictures of helmeted heroes, bat or glove in hand. On the back were rows of statistics, all in fine print, suitable for squinting. They used to have names like Mickey Mantle and Willie Mays. Adults look back and dream about what the present would be like if they'd just hung on to that set of baseball cards from 1962.

Baseball cards are still around, of course, but they've got a lot of company. Now they are called collectibles, and a new craze over them erupts every few years. One of the latest collectible cards doesn't feature baseball players but pudgy cartoon animals (over 150 of them in one of the most popular series today). Each card comes with statistics, and there is a complicated formula for what cards are worth. Collectively, its name is Pokémon, and through it children are learning about the thrill of gambling. The payoff isn't money; it's that one valuable card hidden in among the common cards. Finding one of these cards is like winning the lottery to a child in grade school.

The implications to children caught up in the frenzy of collecting have striking similarities to the winning, losing, and desperation stages of adult gambling. *Time* magazine ran an article that warned of the obsessive tendencies being exhibited by some children involved in collecting cards. "You don't know whether there's a valuable card in a pack when you buy it," says Maressa Hecht Orzack, founder of the Computer Addiction Service at McLean Hospital in Belmont, Massachusetts. "Children under eight aren't able to grasp this fact cognitively, which then leads to disappointment and an increased desire to buy more packs."[2]

Cards like Pokémon are traded by children all over the country. Cards can also be obtained by playing a Pokémon game. With the correct strategy, young people are able to "capture" cards away from their opponent. Pokémon has become so disruptive in some schools, children are prohibited from bringing the cards and trading them at school. Not only did this trading disrupt school activities; it produced behavioral problems because children were preoccupied with the game instead of schoolwork and argued over the outcome of games and trades.

In many ways the problems associated with card crazes of this kind mirror problem gambling. Children are preoccupied with playing the game or trading the cards. A great deal of money is spent hoping to "score" a valuable card, which is against the odds. Peers are viewed as opponents from whom cards can be won or traded. Value is placed on those children with the most valuable cards who obtain bragging rights.

Like all crazes riding the crest of popularity, Pokémon is collapsing under its own weight, destined to sputter and fade as children seek other stimulation. When that happens, across this country there will be boxes under beds and in closets containing stacks and rows of little mutant monster cards, gathering dust and taking up space. The cards will have lost their appeal, but for some children the lure behind the cards will continue. This lure to win, to master, to acquire, to compete, to risk, will find another outlet.

The Entryway of Video Games

Earlier we noted that casinos now provide the stimulation of the adult gambling experience without the monetary payoff. This type of activity is not confined to casino-style gambling establishments. The sights and sounds, bells and whistles, lights and music of those virtual games exist in pizza parlors, convenience stores, and fun zones across the country. Arcade-style video games are now part of childhood.

Many arcades provide tokens or tickets to children who play and win on the games. These tokens or tickets are then redeemed at a prize counter for mere trinkets, representing only a partial value to the amount of money spent acquiring them through playing the games. Cheap prizes require few redemption tickets, and special prizes represent a tremendous monetary outlay for most participants. Scoring big on a game is one way to earn enough tickets for the good prizes. The other way is simply to spend a lot of money. Scoring big is infrequent; spending big is routine.

Video games, which began as an arcade entertainment, have moved closer to home. In fact, they are now in the house. Home gaming systems, hooked up to the family television set or sets, engage children, teenagers, and adults with their intense graphics and professional presentations. The top three—Nintendo, Sega, and Sony—currently vie for the dollars and loyalty of millions of American consumers. These games are compelling, as any parent of an adolescent glued for hours to the television, game controller in hand, can attest.

These are not only games, they are a gateway. In fact, studies show that at-risk and problem adolescent gamblers "are most likely to wager regularly on games of personal skill, card, dice or board games with friends and family, sports and arcade or video games.... The prevalence of at-risk or problem gambling is highest among adolescents who have wagered on arcade or video games."[3]

The experience these games provide is intense, interactive, compelling, and highly competitive—all factors in the addictive nature of adult gambling experiences. Through these games, young people are learning the thrill of this type of stimulation. When actual wagering is added to the potent mix of these games, the pull toward problem gambling behaviors increases.

The Entryway of Bingo

Adolescents are certainly at risk for developing out-of-control gambling habits, but they are by no means the only ones. Adults also need to be aware of how gambling may be drawing them in.

One of the entryways for gambling comes through an unlikely source. Adults are gambling their wages, their Social Security money, and their pensions in church basements and community rooms through a simple game of five letters: B-I-N-G-O. Religious-based organizations discovered this activity as a way to raise funds for worthy causes. Encased within a cocoon of piety, church-based bingo games are no less gambling than the slots at Vegas.

Other organizations have also discovered bingo as a way to generate funds. Community groups and local sports teams are cashing in on gambling dollars by constructing and operating bingo facilities. Payoff percentages are advertised along with the times for the next pancake breakfast.

These gambling establishments represent church and community. It is easy to forget that the proceeds are really profits—dollars gleaned from members of the church or community. It is easy to forget that there are neighbors, community members, and church members who are unable to refrain from placing just one more bet, even though it means they may have to show up at the church on Monday to access the food pantry. Most churches would never dream of opening up a bar to alcoholics, but they are doing the same thing to gamblers by placing a gambling facility in the basement.

The Entryway of Office Pools

As discussed before, office pools are illegal but prevalent. Many of these pools are based on sporting events, but not all. Some track the chances of Mary down in accounting having twins or Bob's beating out Lou for a promotion. These pools can be intricate, nearly incomprehensible charts or informal, word-of-mouth endeavors.

In whatever form, office pools provide people who might not gamble otherwise with a socially acceptable way to place a wager on an unknown outcome. In other words, to gamble in a nongambling setting. In this way, pools act as an entryway for individuals to try gambling out. The thrill of a big win in one of these pools may entice an individual to try her luck elsewhere, in a more recognized gambling setting.

The Entryway of Raffles

For a mere dollar, the buyer has a chance to risk a relatively small amount of money for the chance at a large payoff. If that sounds like a definition of the lottery, it is. It could also be the definition of a raffle. Raffles are common ways for organizations to raise money for their causes. Usually some company donates a prize of considerable value, such as a vacation, a car, or electronic equipment. By purchasing a ticket, individuals risk a small amount of money for a chance at winning the prize. Of course, the more tickets one buys, the more chances one has of winning. Sounds like the lottery, again, doesn't it?

Because raffles are usually for worthy causes, it can be considered philanthropy to buy a ticket. After all, you're helping the local soccer team make it to the playoffs or helping a teen center buy a new Ping-Pong table. Besides, ticket prices are generally low, a dollar or two. Lottery tickets are also low. If a person gets caught up in the excitement of buying a raffle ticket, lotteries provide the next step.

The Entryway of the Internet

The impact of the Internet on established forms of gambling has already been discussed in the previous chapter. As noted, the Internet provides a dizzying array of gambling choices with nearly instantaneous access. Its potency is staggering. Over the Internet, people can play the lottery, play the horses, play the slots. They can also play a new, more subtle form of wagering from an old-style risk-and-reward activity. Day-trading is one of the fastest growing gambling-style entry activities—and one of the most accepted.

Day-trading is the quick-paced purchase and sale of stocks and commodities over the Internet by individual investors. The technology of the Internet allows individuals to gain access to complex trading data, track desired investments, and connect to brokerage houses in order to complete transactions. All of this can be done with the click of a mouse and the buzz of a modem, without interacting with another person.

If someone boasts of winning at a casino, people consider her lucky. If someone boasts of winning at a racetrack, people consider her savvy. If someone boasts of wealth generated through day-trading on the stock market, people consider her shrewd. Day-trading does not carry the negative baggage of more traditional forms of risk. Individuals who might never consider placing a bet on a pony or risking a paycheck on drawing to an inside straight will put substantial sums of money on the line for the latest technology stock. The former is known as gambling; the latter is viewed as business.

Playing the market can prove exciting to someone seeking a thrill. It can prove lucrative to someone seeking money. It can prove empowering to someone seeking control. In fact, without any lingering negative social stigmas, it provides many of the rewards so desperately sought by those who gamble. The rewards are similar to gambling, as are the risks. The money lost through day-trading is just as gone as the money lost through gambling.

RISKY BUSINESS

Many people brush up against gambling without experiencing serious harm. The sheer volume of entry activities, however, ensures that some will cross the line from seemingly harmless fun into the law of unintended consequences. Those unintended consequences can mean a serious problem with gambling. The more varied the entry activities are, the more chances for an individual to come across one that acts as a one-way conduit to compulsive behaviors. When an entry activity becomes the pathway to compulsive gambling, the entryway leads farther and farther from any way out.

WHEN ONE THING LEADS TO ANOTHER

Connie was jittery. Probably too much caffeine, she told herself, hands shaking on the wheel of her car. Clutching the wheel tighter in her left hand, her right hand groped for her purse on the seat. What she really needed was a cigarette, not another cup of coffee. Snagging one out of the pack, she trapped it between her teeth as she glanced over her shoulder and guided the car into the right-hand lane. Her exit was coming up, and she didn't want to miss it.

By the time Connie pulled into the casino parking lot, she was feeling better. Taking deep drags on the cigarette had calmed her down. Once she got inside, there'd be a drink waiting. The servers were trained by now to know just what kind she liked. Connie could taste the vodka as she hurried inside.

A rush of almost sensual pleasure hit her as she thought about the next several hours. The rush was accompanied by a small twinge of guilt. There was truly nothing she liked better than sitting down in front of a row of slots, possibilities beckoning, with a drink in front of her and a cigarette in hand. Brushing the guilt aside, she reminded herself, as she did regularly, that this was her time, her money, her pleasures. What else did she have to look forward to? She deserved this. She had nothing to feel guilty about.

She couldn't wait to get inside.

SPIRAL EFFECT

As Connie's day suggests, addictive behaviors rarely travel alone. When we engage in uncontrolled behavior in one area, we often have difficulty exerting control in other areas. This is especially true if companion behaviors are available with the first compulsive behavior. In his statement to the NGISC, Dr. James Dobson wrote, "There can be no doubt from the evidence that gambling—like many compulsive behaviors—is addictive and progressive in nature."[1] To him, the evidence was clear: Gambling is addictive and, as such, dangerous.

The gambling industry is not blind to the power of linked compulsive behaviors. Industry strategies are designed, in fact, to combine addictive habits. The NGISC recommended that the government look at this strategy more closely, citing that "practices of some gambling facilities to provide free alcohol to customers while gambling, the placement of cash advance credit machines close to the gambling area, and the offer of similar inducements are likely to be significant factors in magnifying or exacerbating a gambling disorder."[2] The more the threads of compulsive behaviors are woven together, the harder the cord is to break and the more tightly the gambler is ensnared.

Gambling and Alcohol

Free or cheap drinks are synonymous with Las Vegas–style casinos. The strategy is well understood by the casinos and by their customers. The customer accepts the drink thinking the free drink is saving him money. The casino offers the drink because it knows the free drink will make money. Gamblers who drink are gamblers who spend more than the price of the alcohol. If this were not the case, the casino would not give it out for free.

Drinking reduces our inhibitions. It impairs our judgment. It causes emotions to supersede logic. All of these conditions encourage the individual to gamble more frequently and for a longer period of time. Many gambling games require strategic thinking, keeping track of the odds, keeping track of the cards, being able to maintain a minimum level of skill to execute the game properly. Alcohol enhances none of this thinking. Gamblers who drink are gamblers who lose.

Drinking is detrimental to gamblers in other ways as well. By linking his gambling experience with another compelling behavior—the consumption of alcohol—a problem gambler is bound even tighter to the source of his gambling problem. According to information provided by the National Council on Problem Gambling, almost half of those identified as pathological gamblers abuse alcohol as well.[3] While gamblers might, at some point, be strong enough to disengage from one addiction, two linked addictions prove almost overwhelming to tackle.

Gambling and Drugs

When gambling moves into a neighborhood, so do drugs. Though extensive research linking narcotics use and gambling has yet to be done, several studies have pointed out disturbing information. In San Jose, California, the police department reported a 200 percent increase in narcotic offenses in the vicinity of a new cardroom.[4]

Perhaps it is not difficult to comprehend a link between a cardroom and narcotics, but what about narcotics and something acceptable like a state-sanctioned lottery? The Washington State study discovered such a link: "There is concern that lottery gambling may be an experience that encourages young people to engage in other, less broadly sanctioned types of gambling as well as in other risk-taking behaviors, such as illicit drug use.… The increase in lottery play is correlated with increased participation in other types of gambling and in use of alcohol, tobacco and marijuana."[5] The study found the higher the frequency of gambling, the higher the chance of a drug or alcohol problem.[6]

Though this study involved adolescents, the same link can be inferred with adults. Gambling is a risk-taking activity. So is using drugs. The willingness to take a risk in one area can be transferred to other areas.

Gambling and Smoking

One of the smells closely associated with a casino floor is cigarette smoke. Cardrooms maintain a perpetual haze above the tables, mingling with the smell of cooked food and spilled drinks.

People who gamble often smoke because smoking produces a sense of calm. In the midst of gambling's risk and uncertainty, a sense of calm is welcome. Getting out a cigarette and lighting it provides familiarity. Smoking is something to occupy the hands and the mouth. It is a way to handle stress and soothe nerves. Nerves and a need to soothe them go hand-in-hand with gambling. Is it any wonder so many gamblers smoke?

Gambling and Improper Eating

Casino locales have always had a reputation for abundant, convenient, cheap food. All-you-can-eat buffets entice gamblers off the gambling floor. They are professionally prepared, efficiently served, and lavishly presented. This might appear to be a contradiction. If gamblers are supposed to be gambling, why would casinos make eating such a pleasure?

The casinos understand gamblers need to eat so they incorporate this need into the total gambling experience. Everything about the current casino layout is designed to produce a suspension of reality for the gambler. Reality includes things like "the odds always favor the house" and "you'll be sorry in the morning." The fantasy experience of the casino perpetuates the myth that ordinary people always win extraordinary amounts of money and an "anything goes" mentality is appropriate for all things, including eating and drinking.

Gamblers are preoccupied with gambling, not food, so they easily fall into the casino fantasy. They are concerned with counting their winnings, not counting calories, with how many pair they have, not their cholesterol level. They are concerned with maintaining their gambling, not maintaining their health. In the rush of the gambling win, eating is irrelevant. If food is available, it's eaten. If it's not, the adrenaline of winning keeps the gambler going. In the despair of a gambling loss, eating can become a consolation. Often alcohol consumption provides the body with a marginal amount of liquid and calories. Smoking inhibits appetite. The total focus on gambling pushes thoughts of hunger and food aside. Once the gambling binge subsides, however, food is either a comfort or a reward. A gambler who loses can't enjoy a win, but he can enjoy a meal. It's small consolation, but a consolation nonetheless. A gambler who wins is apt to celebrate through an excess of food or alcohol or both.

The gambler can abuse food either by eating too little or too much. Whichever the case, food is relegated to an inappropriate status. It is not fuel for the body anymore. It is a nuisance to be deferred, a consolation prize, or an all-you-can-eat reward.

The lack of balance shown in gambling behaviors is mirrored in eating behaviors. Within the casino's artificially created environment, eating and food choices get caught up in make-believe. While all sorts of foods are prepared, health benefits do not always take precedence over rich, calorie-laden delicacies. If the gambler perceives a bargain in purchasing food, the casino calculates he will transfer the savings to an extra bet or three more pulls at the slots. Either way, through the gambling floor or the restaurant one floor up, the casino is betting on capturing the gambler's money.

Gambling and the Internet

As we already outlined, the Internet is proving to be a high-speed electronic conduit through which gambling venues reach out to an expanding group of potential gamblers. The video aspects and virtual reality afforded by Internet technology make Internet gambling attractive and compelling.

In 1997 evidence surfaced at the 104th annual convention of the American Psychological Association that the Internet could be as addicting as alcohol, drugs, and gambling.[7] Since then, additional research has further established a link between using the Internet and uncontrolled behavior patterns.

The Internet by itself is a powerful, compelling medium, capable of producing pathological behavior in a small percentage of those who use it. Gambling is also a powerful, compelling activity, capable of producing pathological behavior in a small percentage of those who participate in it. There are sure to be gamblers who continue or exacerbate their gambling through the Internet. Conversely, there are sure to be Internet users who discover gambling during their forays onto the Web and combine these two potent forces.[8]

Gambling and Sexual Behaviors

Think of the last few ads for a gambling casino or Las Vegas hotel you saw. Besides dice or cards, was there another common denominator? Alongside the roulette wheel on the billboard or accompanying the picture of the latest casino, advertisements for gambling establishments routinely include a picture of a slender, scantily clad show girl. Tottering on stiletto heels, often with an enormous headdress precariously perched, the shapely show girl reflects another effective lure of the gambling industry.

Sex sells and it sells gambling. From the show girl in Las Vegas to the cocktail waitress at the cardroom, sexual stimulation is purposely incorporated into the gambling experience. The Las Vegas strip is known not only for its gambling but also for its prostitution. Sexual arousal is touted as part of the gambling package.

Gamblers can be susceptible to this lure whether they win or lose. A gambler who wins feels special, as if the normal rules do not apply. He may engage in sexual behaviors due to the euphoria of winning. Winners may attract sexual partners who wish to exploit their financial windfall. A gambler who loses feels despondent, vulnerable. He may engage in sexual behaviors due to the despair of losing. Losers may attract sexual partners who wish to exploit their vulnerability.

These sexual liaisons are often impulsive, spur-of-the-moment decisions made during times of heightened emotions. Add alcohol or drugs to this mix, and the ability of the gambler to make responsible sexual choices dramatically declines.

DANGEROUS DOMINOES

When one area of our life spins out of control, it knocks and nudges against the other areas, causing them to wobble off balance. Someone who gambles often finds control of his life slipping away. He starts gambling and ends up drinking. He starts drinking and ends up in bed with a stranger. He ends up in bed with one stranger and ends up in bed with another. He starts gambling and ends up smoking cigarettes. He smokes cigarettes and ends up smoking marijuana. He starts gambling and ends up losing money. He loses money and ends up stealing from work. He steals money from work and ends up getting fired. One choice can lead to other damaging choices, making a long path of destructive behaviors.

1 0

EVANGELICAL
CONSUMERISM

D id you get it?" Beth asked under her breath as she and Marty
headed out the front door of the church.

"Yeah, the most current one," Marty assured her, opening it up and
beginning to flip through the pages, dividing his attention between the
neatly typed columns and the sidewalk in front of him. Gold, this thing
was gold!

At home after lunch, they cleaned off the kitchen table and took
out their newly acquired church directory. With a yellow highlighter
pen, Beth underlined those members she and Marty had met personally.
A pink pen highlighted those they knew of but hadn't yet connected
with at church. A blue pen was used for prospects who still needed to be
checked out. Within a week the yellow group would receive a call from
either Marty or Beth, the pink group would be targeted for personal
contact on Sunday morning, and the blue group would be identified
and further evaluated for suitability.

Marty and Beth had been coming to the church for only a few
months, but they were very friendly and already a favorite for dinners
and game nights. After the first few weeks Marty had shown up at one
of the Saturday morning men's meetings. After a short devotional, it
provided a great way, over pancakes and link sausage, to find out who

did what for work. By the time the devotional was over, breakfast eaten, and the closing prayer offered, Marty knew what every other man in the room did for a living, who was satisfied with his job and who wasn't. He'd been intentionally vague about his own employment; that would come later.

For her part, Beth immediately volunteered to help in the nursery. This put her in contact with the young mothers in the congregation. While they nursed or rocked babies to sleep, she had plenty of time to find out about them, their families, and their lives. Later, she cross-referenced her information with Marty to come up with a list of prospects. Now with the church directory, that list had addresses and phone numbers.

"Hi, this is Marty from church. I was wondering if you'd like to come over to the house on Tuesday night for dinner. There's a great business opportunity Beth and I would love to share with you. I know you've been looking for some extra income, and I really think this would be perfect for you…"

WHEN A DIRECTORY BECOMES A DOWNLINE

Beth and Marty will lead many in their church to a subtle but destructive form of financial temptation that might be defined as gambling itself. Our culture in the past fifty years has produced an interesting entity known as multilevel marketing. In this system, the small percentage of people at the top receive a portion of the proceeds from the work of the vast majority at the bottom. Some have likened this model to a pyramid, not only in shape but also in the way the workers at the bottom level labor for the benefit of the top few.

Those at the bottom level of this model can work their way toward the top by recruiting people to fill in their place at the bottom levels. New people are constantly needed to fill in the ranks of those at the bottom in order to maintain the wedge shape. When a person first enters a multilevel marketing company, she is encouraged to recruit family and friends. If the prospect is leery about the company, her relationship with the person who is already in the company can be enough to persuade her to disregard her initial hesitancy.

Not every person approached, even family and friends, will be interested in the business. For every person who says yes, there will be many others who say no. Therefore, more and more people need to be asked in order to obtain enough who say yes. Once family and friends have been approached and the prospects exhausted from this group, the search must continue.

The answer to this dilemma is to obtain more friends. One of the quickest ways to generate friends is to join a group of people with like interests. For many in the multilevel marketing arena, churches have proven fertile ground for cultivating friends.

Churches are organized around a common set of beliefs and goals. Church members associate with one another, and their religious ties produce an immediate openness and trust. The traditional benefits derived from church associations have always been spiritual and communal in nature. When Beth and Marty show up at church, however, the benefits become financial.

FINANCIAL BLESSINGS

Some people approach the acquisition of wealth with a religious fervor. Some people approach religion with an intense, businesslike pursuit. And some people have found a way to merge religion and business. When the quest for financial freedom meets the desire for spiritual fulfillment, evangelical consumerism is born. When evangelical consumerism through multilevel marketing hits the local church, the church directory can become a downline: a group of people who can be recruited into the business and profited from.

If this perception of multilevel marketing in churches seems far-fetched, or even paranoid, consider these words from Athena Dean in her book *Consumed by Success,* the story of her experiences in multi-level marketing: "In my business, we always taught new recruits that the church was the best place to go to get recruits. One man I know created an entire informational meeting to present at churches. His strategy was to attract one or two sharp individuals who he could get excited about the business. Then they would sell and recruit the rest of the church body. Another woman I knew used to go from church to church, getting involved in women's Bible studies and offering to lead praise and worship. In reality, she was just going to meet new people and find more prospects for her business."[1] Churches provide an established list of people from which business contacts can be gleaned. Those business contacts, in turn, fall into the trap of money's pull.

PERKS AND PITFALLS

In many ways this brand of evangelical consumerism mirrors the benefits and pitfalls of gambling without anyone ever picking up a pair of dice or pulling on a one-armed bandit. The benefits are obvious—money and the control and sense of self-worth having money brings. The pitfalls of multilevel marketing also mimic those of gambling: obsession with the activity itself, financial hardship, alienation from friends and family, and a loss of perspective.

Multilevel marketing imitates gambling in another important area. Just as gamblers are initially hooked by a big win, those drawn to multilevel marketing are similarly snared by initial success. However, just as gambling losses consume winnings, multilevel marketing expenses can gobble up earnings. Athena Dean puts it this way: "Even though by this time we were cash-flowing $50,000 a year, our overhead was so high that we were perpetually broke.... Even when we hit the coveted $100,000 mark, our expenses far exceeded our income."[2] As in gambling, the individual becomes consumed trying to repeat that first flush of success, chasing faster and faster after the carrot of financial independence.

The perk of this style of business is money. The hook is the promise that, after the initial effort, the money will come pouring in through the work of others. Their success is your success. Their hard work is your reward for recruiting them into the business. Wealthy individuals and couples higher up in the business give testimony to the financial rewards by showcasing cars, boats, and recreational vehicles, all obtained through their percentage checks. The levels these lofty people inhabit have names like "emerald, " "ruby," "pearl," and "diamond." Each costly gemstone invokes the building blocks of heaven on earth for those farther down the line, if not the very composition of the road to heaven itself.

The pitfalls of this style of business can be far from heavenly: financial ruin, emotional exhaustion, alienation of relationships, and a loss of perspective. The vast majority of people who become involved with multilevel marketing do not profit from it. Engineer Bradley Orner was involved in Amway, one of the major multilevel marketing businesses, for three and a half years. According to Orner, only one-half of 1 percent of those involved with Amway reach the higher levels and the financial rewards the higher levels bring. Using a gross-versus-net income formula, he calculates that over 95 percent of those involved in Amway actually lose money each month.[3]

Chasing after the dream of financial independence, either through a business or an activity such as gambling, is emotionally draining. As with gambling, in multilevel marketing there is an initial adrenaline rush. This rush is perpetuated by the waiting and hoping for the next big check or the next on-fire recruit. These are inevitably met with the letdown of dashed hopes, people saying no, less-than-anticipated earnings and greater-than-expected expenses. These up-and-down roller coaster rides of emotion eventually drain a person of her reason and mental equilibrium, reflecting the type of mood swings of elation and despair common with problem gamblers.

For gamblers, family and friends become just another source of needed cash. For those heavily involved in multilevel marketing, family and friends are either in the business and thus a source of revenue, or not in the business and thus a source of bitter disappointment. Coupling relationships with revenue is destructive. It alienates loved ones, as they rightly feel used for financial reasons by either the gambler or the multi-level marketer. Gamblers will cajole family and friends into loaning them money, promising to pay them back with interest from their expected winnings. Multilevel marketers work family members into the business, promising them financial rewards from profits. As family and friends soon find out, gamblers rarely win and multilevel marketing businesses rarely show the level of return promised. With promises left unfulfilled, relationships suffer.

Relationships with others suffer through these activities, as does the individual's relationship with reality. Perception becomes skewed. The business of winning or the business of business takes on a disproportionate importance in the mind of the individual. Behaviors and attitudes are rationalized. Greed is viewed as initiative. Using other people is viewed as sharing opportunity. Continually overworking is viewed as temporarily necessary. Worth is calculated by monetary value. Caught within this warped perception, damaging behaviors appear justified and even noble.

SPIRITUAL AND FINANCIAL FERVOR

It is ironic that this style of business is so prevalent among God's people. For many, the evangelical fervor for a spiritual experience is echoed in the quest for financial freedom. These two very opposite things often incestuously merge in churches through multilevel marketing.

The Bible is clear that a person cannot love God and love money. However, many Christians believe they can bribe God to overlook their love for money if they contribute part of this money to the church. Their own greed is justified as a sincere desire to see God's kingdom furthered through their monetary offerings. Because a portion of the proceeds of their business is being funneled into the church, church members are seen as fair game for recruitment into the business. Often, the ability to have extra money to "give to the church" is used as a recruitment tool. Giving back a portion of the proceeds to the church is seen as ensuring God's stamp of approval on this activity.

Multilevel marketing can appear to Christians as a sanitized, sanctified source of gambling-style stimulation and rewards. Those of us who would never consider going to Vegas or stopping at a cardroom on our way home from church can become ensnared in it without realizing the pitfalls that accompany the perks.

11

WHEN THE LUCK RUNS OUT

The scene is familiar: a meeting at a suburban city hall with local officials facing fiscal restraints. As they look over the budget for the next year, they see that the costs of providing essential city services keep rising. Past experience tells them that the citizens are reluctant to give approval for increased taxes. State money is getting harder and harder to come by. Faced with these realities, they see parks receiving less maintenance, libraries closed longer hours, police protection spread thinner, and city fees going higher.

Further down the meeting agenda is discussion of a zoning change application for an abandoned piece of property a few blocks off the interstate. It's a piece of property well known to the group. Thirty years ago, it housed a grocery store. As the surrounding area changed from residential to commercial, its base of shoppers shifted away. For five years the building has stood vacant. Plywood boards cover the windows. Weeds work their way up through the fractured asphalt and tumble over old planting strip curbs. Police are called in regularly to chase off vagrants or groups of teenagers drawn to its litter-strewn interior.

Now a group of out-of-state businesses are interested in purchasing the property and constructing a brand-new restaurant and cardroom. They promise to completely renovate the property, add sidewalks

around the exterior, a streetlight at the intersection, and attractive land-
scaping. They pledge to make it a priority to hire locals, for both the ren-
ovation work and for the employees after the job is finished.

Each city official is given a packet outlining the proposal and the
changes promised. Included are colored renderings of what the new
building and grounds will look like. The facade is modern and clean.
Trees and vegetation give it a parklike appeal. Attached on thick parch-
ment paper is a crisp list of the type and number of jobs to be brought
into the community by the new business. Highlighted prominently at
the bottom is the amount of projected tax revenue to be generated by
the business and deposited into the city coffers.

On one side of the table is the city official most excited about the
new project. He's spoken with the representatives from the consortium
and eagerly reminds the others in the room of the benefits of the project.
On the other side of the table is the city official most suspicious about
the new project. She is just as eager as he to have a solution to the eyesore
cluttering up the city's industrial core, but she has concerns about the
nature of the business. As the two of them debate and discuss back and
forth, the rest of the city officials remain in the middle, unsure of which
side will win, unsure of which side should win.

PANDORA'S BOX

What thirty years ago was considered unsuitable for inclusion in communities—especially suburban and bedroom communities—is now
considered suitable and, in some cases, even desirable. Dazzled by the
sums of money generated by gambling businesses, many communities
are opening up a Pandora's box when they allow the construction of
gambling venues. Jobs are promised. Economic recovery is heralded.
Increased revenues are allotted for worthwhile endeavors, like schools.
But under that shiny surface lie dark consequences: increased crime,

personal financial ruin, divorce, domestic violence and neglect, homelessness and unemployment, and suicide.

In order to make wise decisions about gambling in our communities and our own lives, we need to be aware of gambling's effects. We also need to be aware of the practical help and God-given hope available to our broken families and neighborhoods. Below are listed some of the ways gambling can destroy us; in the next section we will learn what we can do about it.

Increased Crime

San Jose, California, faced a decision regarding a cardroom. They decided to invite the business into their community. In the year after the cardroom opened its doors, the police department looked into the impact on the surrounding area. Traffic accidents had increased by 55 percent. Auto theft was up 21 percent. Property crimes of all kinds went up by 83 percent in the area around the cardroom, with petty theft up 56 percent. The highest increase went to narcotics offenses, discussed in an earlier chapter, which rose by a staggering 200 percent in a single year.[1]

San Jose is not alone. The previous example, as well as the following examples of the criminal impact of gambling on communities, are from a Focus on the Family Research report on gambling and crime:[2]

- After casinos opened in Atlantic City, the total number of crimes within a thirty-mile radius increased by over 100 percent.[3]
- In the five years after the Foxwoods Casino opened in Ledyard, Connecticut, the number of calls to its police department quadrupled from 4,000 a year to 16,700 a year.[4]
- The police department in the quiet town of Black Hawk, Colorado, used to receive around 25 calls a year. Then casinos went in. Now the annual number of calls to the Black Hawk Police Department runs between 15,000 to 20,000.[5]

- University of Nevada at Las Vegas researchers, a group well positioned to understand the influence of gambling, conducted a study for the Wisconsin Policy Research Institute on the effects on crime due to casino gambling in that state. They concluded the presence of casinos in the state of Wisconsin brings an average of 5,300 additional major crimes each year, as well as an additional 17,100 arrests for minor crimes.[6]

Ask a city official, concerned with economic growth in the community, if bringing in a gambling venue or casino will be positive for the community, and he may answer yes. Ask a law enforcement official, concerned with the safety and protection of the community he serves, if bringing in that same gambling venue or casino will be positive for the community, and he will probably answer no. Across the country, the evidence is available for drawing a definitive link between the introduction of gambling and increased crime.

Personal Financial Ruin

When gambling venues come to town, revenue is generated from gamblers. Most gamblers control their gambling and do not spend beyond what they can afford. Some gamblers, however, especially those who gamble regularly, are unable to balance their gambling expenditures with their income. The National Opinion Research Council (NORC) survey of 530 patrons at gambling facilities, specifically conducted for the NGISC, showed that more than 13 percent of regular gamblers "met the lifetime criteria for pathological or problem gambling, while another 18 percent were classified as 'at risk' for developing severe gambling problems."[7] Add those two figures together and we learn that almost a third of those who gambled regularly had, or were at risk to have, problems associated with their gambling.

One of the severe consequences that surfaces in the life of a compulsive gambler is ruined finances, followed by the necessity to declare bankruptcy. According to the National Research Council for the Academy of the Sciences: "Bankruptcy presents yet another adverse consequence of excessive gambling. In one of the few studies to address bankruptcy [researchers] found that 28 percent of the 60 pathological gamblers attending Gamblers Anonymous reported either that they had filed for bankruptcy or reported debts of $75,000 to $150,000."[8] According to statistics from the National Council on Problem Gambling, the average amount of debt incurred by an American male pathological gambler is between about $55,000 to $90,000. The average debt for an American female pathological gambler is almost $15,000.[9]

How can someone wind up so far into debt? The answer is fairly simple—credit. According to the NORC, lines of credit are a normal business practice for the casino industry: "Not surprisingly, the largest casinos averaged almost 19,000 customers who had been issued a line of credit, a much higher figure than among the smaller or the tribal casinos. Most of the casinos were in states in which gambling debts were enforceable in state courts. Of those that are not in these states, the average amount that had gone uncollected was $157,287 distributed across an average of about eighty-four customers (almost $1,900 per customer)."[10]

Not only do casinos and other gambling establishments issue lines of credit to gamblers, they make available cash machines at or near the gambling location. This was such an area of concern for the NGISC, the commissioners included this recommendation: "Because the easy availability of automated teller machines and credit machines encourages some gamblers to wager more than they intended, the Commission recommends that states, tribal governments, and pari-mutuel facilities ban credit card cash advance machines and other devices activated by debit or credit cards from the immediate area where gambling takes place."[11] Caught up in the rush of the moment, problem gamblers impulsively activate cash machines or lines of credit in order to continue to gamble, stressing their finances when they attempt to pay off those debts.

Divorce

Financial strains brought on by compulsive gambling behaviors and excessive gambling debt produce marital strain. In the NORC study, over half (53.5 percent) of those identified as pathological gamblers said they were divorced. By comparison, the figure was 29.8 percent for those identified as low-risk gamblers and 18.2 percent for those who didn't gamble at all. Gambling was cited in the NORC study as "a significant factor" in a prior divorce.[12]

When gambling consumes a spouse, more than money is diverted to support the gambler's addictive behavior. The gambling spouse also spends time just thinking about gambling. Attention, energy, and devotion are transferred from the spousal relationship to the gambling relationship. It becomes not a matter of another woman or man but another love—the love of gambling. The stress on the relationship eventually fractures the marriage bonds. One witness, testifying to the NGISC about the divorce from her gambler husband, said, "I was compelled to divorce their father, a compulsive gambler. Divorce is one of the most painful things that we, as adults, sometimes must face. Yet, without divorce, I am very much in doubt that I would have skirted a complete mental breakdown."[13]

The Washington State Council on Problem Gambling lists the "high incidence of marital discord" as a result of problem gambling.[14] As gamblers go deeper and deeper into the losing phase of their addiction, the amount of money lost to gambling increases, as does the amount of time given to gambling. Left outside, the rest of the family suffers. At some point, the gambler's spouse may decide the relationship is beyond repair and end the marriage.

Domestic Violence and Neglect

Before a marriage dies completely, those caught in its death throes are injured. The NGISC discovered that one of the most tragic consequences of problem and pathological gambling was damage done to families through domestic violence and child neglect. "Clearly," the report states, "the extent of personal consequences on the pathological gambler and his or her family may be severe, including domestic violence, child abuse, and financial hardships."[15]

When a gambler is losing, he is angry, desperate. In the downward spiral of compulsive addiction and severe financial hardship, he can experience intense bouts of rage and despair. Unfortunately, the gambler may choose to vent these intense, negative emotions on family members in the form of physical abuse. According to one woman from Biloxi, Mississippi: "I lived in fear daily due to his agitation and outbursts of violence: broken doors, overturned furniture, broken lamps, walls with holes in them. I haven't the words to describe the hell that my life became on a daily basis."[16]

Not only can children suffer physical abuse from a gambling parent, they can also suffer the abuse of neglect. Some children are simply left at home when their parent or parents are away gambling. Other children are left inside locked cars for extended periods of time. The NGISC cites the deaths of two children locked in cars while their parents gambled. In a study of ten casino communities, six communities cited an increase in child neglect due to gambling. Respondents "attributed this increase at least in part to parents leaving their children alone at home or in casino lobbies and parking lots while they went to gamble."[17] In the reckless pursuit of their gambling behaviors, some pathological gamblers endanger the lives of their children in exchange for a few moments more in front of the slot machines, at the blackjack table, or in front of video poker.

Homelessness and Unemployment

Once a gambler's compulsive behavior damages his family beyond repair, what happens to the gambler? Many end up homeless. When eleven hundred clients at rescue missions all across the country were asked the reason for their homelessness, 18 percent said it was due to their gambling.[18] As gambling destroys the relationship structures in their lives, many are left without a home to go to.

Unemployment exacerbates homelessness among gamblers. As gambling and thinking about gambling take up more and more of the gambler's time and energy, productivity at his workplace diminishes. The severe mood swings prevalent in problem gamblers sour working relationships and erect barriers to employers and coworkers trying to help. Many people simply cease to try to deal with a difficult and unreliable employee, and the gambler will lose his job. Unemployment among problem gamblers is considerably higher than in the general population.[19] Without a home to go to or a job to count on, some pathological gamblers wind up living on the streets.

Suicide

The weight of despair over gambling problems can be enough to crush anyone's spirit. For some people involved with pathological gambling, death seems the only way out. The following are statistics from the National Council on Problem Gambling:

- Pathological gamblers have a suicide rate that is twenty times higher than nongamblers.
- One in five pathological gamblers attempts suicide.
- The suicide rate for pathological gamblers is higher than for any other addictive disorder.
- Eleven percent of problem gamblers' wives attempt suicide.

What state regularly reports the highest rate of suicide? Nevada. In 1995 the suicide rate in Nevada was more than twice the national average.[20] A survey of almost four hundred Gamblers Anonymous members showed that two-thirds had contemplated suicide. Almost half had a definite plan to end their lives, and over three-fourths expressed a desire to die.[21]

The police departments in Atlantic City, Reno, and Las Vegas are frequently needed to respond to visitors who decide to end their lives because of gambling.[22] The chamber of commerce calls tourists to gamble; the police are called when some tourists lose too much.

A Life of Crime

Few problem or pathological gamblers determine early on to engage in lives of crime. But like drug addicts, some gamblers will turn to illegal activities to finance their gambling. Sixty-five percent of pathological gamblers commit crimes to support their gambling habit.[23] Consider the following statistics of gamblers who admit to committing crimes:

- 34 percent write bad checks
- 31 percent take out loans and then don't repay them
- 30 percent steal from their employers through embezzlement
- 20 percent commit forgery
- 19 percent evade paying taxes
- 12 percent fill out fraudulent tax information[24]

When gamblers are caught in their crimes, an additional societal cost is paid along with the cost of a devastated family and a ruined life. Often the community bears the legal—and the correctional—costs of dealing with those gamblers who commit money-related crimes to support their gambling.

When the luck runs out, everybody loses.

GAIN VS. LOSS

Communities seek the monetary gain produced by gambling venues. Those dollars are quantifiable in terms of increased employment, revenue, and taxes. The costs to a community for allowing gambling is harder to define. The NGISC called this aspect of their endeavor "the most troubling...beyond dollar amounts, how does one quantify a divorce, a loss of life savings, or worse, a gambling-induced suicide?"[25]

If the average person is asked whether he believes there is a link between gambling activities and an increase in crime, he will answer no.

On the other hand, that same person believes there is a link between gambling activities and an increase in community revenue. Therein lies the dilemma. As the NGISC reports, "The key question is this: How do gambling's benefits measure against its costs?"[26] Even after two years of extensive research, the question cannot be definitively answered. The overall amount of high-quality and relevant research in this area is still extremely limited.

The negative influences of gambling's Pandora's box have only recently become recognizable. As we learn more, we must each decide— as communities and as individuals—whether the rewards of gambling outweigh the risks. In the next section we'll highlight some practical ways we can make that decision.

Section 2 Follow-Up

As humans, a constant battle between good and evil wars within us. We desire to do good, but we do evil. The apostle Paul, writing in Romans, put it this way: "For I have the desire to do what is good, but I cannot carry it out. For what I do is not the good I want to do; no, the evil I do not want to do—this I keep on doing" (Romans 7:18-19).

Every temptation has a moment of greatest vulnerability when the decision to do right or to do wrong is made. Sometimes circumstances beyond our control present us with that choice. Our culture used to assist us in resisting gambling. As a whole, our cultural values weighed in on the side against gambling. Much of the gambling that did take place was done within families or groups of people who knew each other. In such a setting there were people who cared about us who could see if a problem arose and could intervene. Gambling was also not as accessible. People needed to plan to gamble, and some of the most popular forms of gambling today didn't even exist.

While the culture has changed, God and his help have not. We have the opportunity to receive God's help for our community and our home.

Whether you are a gambler yourself or are concerned for a gambler you know, take some time to consider the following questions. In the first section, you looked inward to evaluate your own feelings regarding gambling and needs. This time, look outward—at the culture we live in—and evaluate how you have been influenced by that culture.

If you are working in a group, after you have answered the questions on your own, compare notes on how you see gambling's influence in your immediate culture. Talk about how you as individuals can respond to that influence.

Follow-up Questions

1. Think back to when you were introduced to gambling. Where was it? Who was gambling, and how were you related to them? Do you remember it as a positive or negative experience?

2. What do you see in your immediate neighborhood that encourages gambling? Do you consider this to be a danger?

3. Think about how advertising presents gambling. Try to remember any television commercials, radio spots, or newspaper ads that have caught your eye in the past. What did those ads really promise? What were they really selling? Were they effective in making you consider gambling?

4. In what ways do you see television programs—sitcoms, soap operas, game shows—treat the subject of gambling? Is gambling considered positive, negative, something to laugh about? How does this reflect our culture's perceptions of gambling?

5. In what ways are some of the subtle "entry" activities that might lead to problem gambling—office pools, casual sports bets, collectible cards—part of your life? Do these activities ever lead you to want to gamble more, or do you feel you are able to keep them in check? At what point (if ever) do you believe these activities cross the line to be destructive—for you personally, for your children, for your church?

6. What addictions have you observed in conjunction with gambling? These could be your own, those you have seen, or those you know about. Do you have the impression that those other behaviors are enhanced by gambling and vice versa?

7. What is your church's attitude toward gambling? Does your church promote any activity that you feel might be harmful to some church members? Have you or someone you know ever justified gambling behaviors because they were part of church business?

8. Have you ever thought about what you would do if you won the lottery? Have you ever calculated in your mind what you would do with it? Write down what you would do if you won ten million dollars. Be specific in your answers.

9. Look at what you wrote in response to the last question. How did you feel as you were answering? Did it make you feel excited to think about? Has that excitement ever prompted you to purchase a lottery ticket or engage in some other form of gambling?

10. Think about the negative aspects of gambling. In your opinion, do the benefits of gambling outweigh the negatives?

11. If you could bring back one thing that formerly kept gambling in check in our culture, what would it be and why?

12. One of the best ways for Christians to determine how the culture is influencing them, instead of the other way around, is to go back to our template for behavior, Jesus. Spend some time considering the question of our day: How do you think Jesus would respond to our culture's acceptance of gambling? How do you think he would respond to a gambler who has lost hope?

13. Spend some time in prayer, seeking God's help in realigning your heart, soul, and mind to the image of Jesus. As you envision how you would look, act, and feel if you acted in accordance with Jesus, what part does gambling play in that realignment?

SECTION 3

PRACTICAL HOPE AND HELP

In section 1 we looked at individual gamblers and why some people are prone to gambling. We can see in them struggles we all face. In section 2 we came face to face with our complicit culture. Though no overarching societal scheme emerged orchestrating a national surge in gambling, decisions and attitudes promoted by our culture have "greased the skids" for gambling's wild ride to prominence.

In both sections we looked at what individuals have to say about gambling, what governments have to say about gambling, and what society has to say about gambling. Ultimately, it doesn't matter what people think or what governments decree or what culture dictates—God alone has the final word on this subject.

Why should God care whether people gamble—why should God care about anything we do? God cares because of his unfailing love for us. People fail. Behaviors they thought they could control overwhelm them. For the Christian who gambles excessively, the temptation to gamble takes over the desire to live a godly life. Yes, people fail—God's people fail—but God is faithful. As Psalm 46:1 beautifully reminds us, "God is our refuge and strength, an ever-present help in trouble."

For some people, including Christians, control over gambling is an overwhelming struggle. The only thing "ever-present" in their lives seems to be the trouble. Culture can no longer be counted on to help rein in gambling behaviors. Family and friends may have grown apathetic to the struggle, even leaving the battlefield completely. Survey the damage caused by compulsive gambling—to individuals, to communities, to the fabric of society itself—and there is little to lead us to hope.

Hope lives, however. It lives and breathes in the promises of God and in the presence of the Holy Spirit. This hope is available to all of us. Gambling is not a challenge too big for God; God is bigger than our problems. Rescuing a problem gambler is not a task begrudgingly undertaken by God; he is the one who rescues us from the pit. Redeeming one of his beloved children from the grips of a terrible compulsion is not a fight God shrinks from; he is a compassionate Father, prepared to fight for his children. Section 3 will help you be prepared, as well.

HOPE FOR THE OCCASIONAL GAMBLER

Yep, can't wait," Mel said, as he expertly loaded the cans of green beans, fruit cocktail, and chili into the bottom of the grocery sack. "Going to Vegas next week."

"You go every three or four months, don't you?" his customer asked while filling out her check.

"Yep, wouldn't miss it." He made sure to put the loaf of bread carefully on the top of the sack, not to squish it. "I catch the red-eye after work on Friday and, with a personal day, don't have to be back to the grind until Tuesday afternoon. Works out great. It's my way of unwinding, you know, blowin' off a little steam." He lifted up the filled bag and deposited it in the grocery cart to his left.

The customer just nodded, tearing off the check and handing it to Mel. She didn't want to say anything, but really she found flying to Las Vegas that often a little…well, excessive. She wondered if maybe Mel had a gambling problem. Hard to tell from the look of him, she decided to herself, gathering up her things.

"Oh!" she said to Mel suddenly, pulling her wallet back out of her purse. "I almost forgot! The jackpot's up to twelve million. Ring me up five lottery tickets, okay?"

HOW MUCH IS TOO MUCH?

Recreational or leisure activities are pleasurable and have a way of overtaking more mundane responsibilities. Whether we enjoy watching television or surfing the Internet or reading, some of us face the ongoing question: "How much is too much?" The quick answer might be that it's too much when that activity takes on an inappropriate importance in my life. When I'd rather be watching television than spending time with a friend, it's too much. When I'd continually rather be surfing the Internet than working at my job, it's too much. When I'd always rather be reading about someone else's life than living my own, it's too much.

The same question needs to be asked about gambling, even when the person doing the asking considers herself to be just an occasional gambler like Mel. If we gamble a small amount of money, or if considerable time elapses between gambling events, we often assume our gambling is not a problem. However, the occasional gambler has other factors to consider when evaluating the effect of her gambling.

Intensity
When evaluating whether our gambling or another person's gambling is a problem, it is tempting to look only at the frequency of the gambling experience. While this is certainly a factor to be considered, another factor not to be overlooked is the intensity of the gambling experience. Just because a person is not devoting significant hours each week to actual gambling does not mean she is free from gambling's pull. All aspects of a person's gambling need to be evaluated to determine whether or not she is addicted.

Adding It Up
The amount of money wagered does not necessarily indicate whether someone's gambling has gone out of control. For example, one person

might wager a large sum on the outcome of a sporting event on a whim, caught up in the excitement of the moment. If that person wins she may laugh, be relieved, and be reminded of how easily the outcome could have been different.

Another person might set aside a comparatively small amount of money each week to purchase lottery tickets or get a scratch card. Over time, however, these small amounts of money will overtake the sum represented by the larger wager. The consistent, unwavering pattern of purchase may speak louder than the one-time wager, warning of that person's inability to control her gambling.

Attitudes

It is also important to look at a person's attitudes about gambling. In other words, even when she is not gambling, does she still think about gambling? Does she still talk about those gambling experiences? Does she dwell on her losses? Does she want to repeatedly relive the thrill of winning? Does she devote a significant amount of time and energy planning when she will gamble again?

Because of outside circumstances or self-imposed restrictions, a person addicted to gambling may not spend a great deal of time actually gambling. Part of the allure of gambling for that person may be the anticipation and preparation surrounding the gambling experience itself. The moment before a wager still holds all of the promise of what's possible. For this person, it is the promise of the possible, as much as the outcome, that fuels her desire to gamble.

In short, it is important to look at whether or not gambling is a sporadic, separated event or an integrated life experience. Most Americans at present fall into the former category in their gambling. However, the latter category increasingly claims more and more of us. When gambling becomes incorporated into the fabric of a person's life, the more difficult it is to separate out.

Words to the Occasional Gambler

If you have picked up this book and identify yourself as an occasional gambler, you may have spent a great deal of time distancing yourself from the extreme behavior discussed here. It is tempting to say, "Yes, but that's not me!" And you may be correct—for now.

As with any activity, there is always a choice. After reading what you have so far regarding gambling and its effects on individuals and communities, you have a personal choice about whether to continue to gamble, even occasionally. Reading this book, answering the questions, and evaluating your own actions may have given you the reassurance you seek concerning the level of risk in your gambling. You may be saying to yourself, right now, "Good! I've got this under control."

If that is the case, congratulations. If there's not a doubt in your mind that gambling is harmless as far as you're concerned, have fun and enjoy.

If, however, reading this book has started that little voice inside your head wondering if gambling is becoming a problem, take the time to reflect on your attitude toward gambling. Take the time to evaluate not only how you gamble but how you feel about gambling. Be honest with yourself and dig below the surface for the root of your doubts.

First Steps

The first thing you can do to evaluate the depth of your desire to gamble is to stop. You needn't put any sort of time limit on this moratorium; just decide to stop whatever gambling you're currently engaged in. If it's buying lottery tickets every week, quit. If it's hopping on the Internet at night and connecting to a casino-type Web site, don't. If it's meeting friends at the track or at the riverboat for drinks and a night of gambling, invite them over to your house instead. If it's heading up the interstate to the tribal casino on Fridays, stay home. Wait to see how long it takes for you to miss your gambling.

Once you have begun to miss your gambling, write down how often you think about gambling. Put down the emotions you are feeling as you remind yourself you're not going to be doing that for now. Write down also if your mind begins to present you with reasons why it would be perfectly acceptable for you to forgo your self-imposed restriction on gambling.

As you work through your feelings, be sure to notice and write down any odd, out-of-place emotions or impressions that come to you. Whether you are aware of it or not, your occasional gambling could have been used to obscure other thoughts or emotions, such as fear, anger, or insecurity. These thoughts or emotions will emerge from behind the shadow of your gambling the longer you refrain from gambling. You might also record any dreams or nightmares you experience during this time. These will prove insightful.

You may find you are able to stop gambling without experiencing anxiety. If so, consider giving it up altogether for the sake of those around you. If it doesn't mean that much to you, be aware of those around you for whom it may have an inappropriate meaning. How tragic it would be for something that caused you no problem at all to become a cause of great distress for someone you care about, now or in the future.

You may find you are surprised at how quickly feelings of deprava-tion and panic set in as you commit yourself to forgo gambling. You may also find yourself surprised at the twists and turns of logic you come up with to try to justify wavering on your commitment to dig deeper into the parameters of your gambling. Be prepared to come to terms with the realization that gambling is really more important to you than you thought. Be prepared also to spend some time and energy discovering why.

Personal Inventory
This is an excellent time for you to take stock of who you are, to use this as a way to do a personal inventory. Personal inventories can be done at

any time and for a variety of reasons, but your investigation of your gambling and how it affects you may be the right time for you to open up and be honest with yourself. Through reading this book, you may have discovered a measure of self-deception in how you look at your gambling. Be honest with yourself. (The Gambling Personality Questionnaire is provided as a tool for you to use for this personal inventory.)

Truth can be difficult to swallow. You may discover that your gambling behaviors have been a way for you to deal with negative emotions in the present or negative experiences in the past. Once you have faced that truth, however, you can begin to put those negative thoughts behind you. By facing the truth instead of running from it, you can move beyond the pain toward healing.

One of the hardest things we face is our own imperfection. We spend so much time crafting a polished image to represent to the world, sometimes we begin to believe in our own creation. Once we are deceived into looking at ourselves through the lens of a polished image, others can appear very flawed indeed. It becomes comforting to look at the problems, predicaments, and foibles of others, knowing they will never touch us. We can spend so much time looking outward, we never take the time to look inward.

If you are gambling, even occasionally, take the time to look inward. Evaluate not only how you are gambling, but why. If the reasons uncover a flaw in your own character or behavior, face that truth. Allow the reminder of your imperfect nature to activate your sense of humility. Recognizing your own imperfections allows you to have empathy for the imperfections in others. Allow the reminder of your imperfect nature to activate your sense of gratitude. Recognizing your own imperfections will fuel your thankfulness in the forgiveness and grace of God.

You need not stop, however, just recognizing your imperfections. Restoration should always follow recognition. It is possible, with God's help, to use this personal insight as a foundation for ongoing personal growth and renewal. If you have discovered that gambling has a greater hold over you than you have been willing to admit, don't throw up your hands and give up.

Next Steps

If you discover that you are struggling to stop gambling, do not continue to face that struggle alone. Immediately find a caring family member or friend to confide in. Choose an appropriate listener, someone who can bring wisdom and hope while really listening to you. Speak honestly and openly about what you are discovering. Pray for strength and accept wise, godly counsel.

Be open to seeking competent, caring professional help. Gambling is only one of many addictive behaviors that can overtake a person. There are proven, effective ways to successfully extricate yourself from an addictive pattern, whether newly established or deeply entrenched. Professional counselors and therapists are trained in these ways and can assist you in developing the tools you need to rein in activities that have, or will, become out of control.

WORDS TO A FRIEND OR LOVED ONE

Maybe gambling has no sway over your own life but you are concerned about the effect it has on someone you love. If you are concerned enough to pick up and read this book, you must have noticed something about another's behavior that was upsetting or troubling to you. Maybe you even confronted that person with her behavior to no avail.

Don't be discouraged. Work through the issue of your loved one's gambling just for yourself if necessary, until you have come up with an answer to the question of whether your loved one has a problem. If she does not have a problem, that person should at least be grateful for your care and concern. If she does have a problem, that person may not be able to see it. In the midst of her struggle, she will need you to provide her with clarity and insight.

Evaluating whether your loved one has a problem is similar to the self-evaluation done by the occasional gambler (just outlined). You do the personal inventory with the gambler in mind. The closer you are to the gambler, the easier this will be. Observe the gambler, providing concrete examples to support your answers.

If you are convinced a problem exists with your loved one's gambling behavior, remember that your conviction may not be enough to persuade her to give up or modify her gambling. That is her choice. Several barriers may make it difficult for the gambler to accept that a problem exists.

Timing

It's important to consider whether a person is ready to change before we try to modify someone's behavior. Present a truth to a person when she is not ready to hear it, and she won't hear it. If the windows of her heart are boarded up because of denial, you can knock all you want with the truth of your conviction and she simply will not open up.

After doing the self-evaluation and thinking and praying through the issue, you may know what you want to say. You also need to be sensitive to when to say it. Your timing will not be effective if your loved one is not ready to listen. Instead of bringing you closer together, raising the issue could set off alarms in the other person that damage your relationship. If you are prayerfully sensitive about this issue of timing, rest in God's assurance that he will give you wisdom and grace for when you do choose to speak up.

Fear

If you are convinced your loved one has a problem, don't panic. Don't allow your fear to overtake your concern for her. Your desire to fix her problem, as you see it, and relieve your own sense of anxiety about her welfare can become overwhelming. You care about her and want her to be better—now.

If you sense fear and impatience is controlling your perception of how to confront the gambler, you might try a more subtle approach. Instead of confronting the person immediately and demanding that she stop gambling, try gauging whether you can persuade her to refrain from gambling without confrontation. For example, if she buys lottery tickets every week, would she be willing to take that money for a month and donate it to a worthy cause she supports? Offer the person who hops on the Internet every Tuesday night a different activity—one you know she will enjoy—as an alternative. If your friend occasionally goes to a casino or riverboat to gamble, invite her out to dinner or to another interactive outing instead.

It will become evident quickly just how important your loved one's particular gambling activity is. If you don't succeed the first time, keep trying different ways to distract her from her gambling. The harder she is to distract, the more deeply entrenched her gambling is. If and when the timing is right to confront her about her gambling, you will have specific incidents and evidence to offer to support your concern.

Hostility

At some point the gambler you are worried about will probably catch on to what you are doing. When that moment comes, don't lie—be honest. Explain your concern over her gambling. Her reaction to discovering this will indicate how much of a problem gambling is. Watch for a defensive, hostile attitude.

Some people get defensive and hostile whenever their actions are called into question, whether there is a problem or not. This could be the case with the person you are concerned about. Your demonstration of love and concern for this person should be enough to convince her of your good intentions. If the hostility remains even after you have showed your concern, you may have tapped into feelings of anxiety and loss when she thinks about reducing the gambling behavior. This reaction is a strong sign of a gambling problem.

One Thing at a Time

Your first concern is to try to determine if there is a problem. If you believe there is a problem, your next job is to communicate your concern clearly and compassionately in a timely manner. On the other hand, after you have observed the person you are concerned about, you may conclude that no problem exists. In that case, relax, and don't hyperventilate when she buys a raffle ticket from the next neighborhood kid.

You may conclude the occasional gambler you are concerned about has no significant problem for the time being. In other words, after observing her behavior, you do not believe her to have a problem now, but you have some doubt in your mind about the potential for a problem developing in the future. In that case, remain alert. Watch and, most of all, make yourself available to your loved one. If you show love and concern in all areas of her life and are open to her confiding in you, the occasional gambler you are concerned about will be more willing to come to you if she senses a problem arising. If your loved one has confidence in your relationship, this person will listen to you if you feel it necessary to confront her with your growing concern.

After all is said and done, you may become convinced that your occasional gambler is really a compulsive gambler just waiting for the right circumstances. Prayerfully, carefully, with love, share your concerns with her. Make sure to communicate compassion, not condemnation. Indicate your willingness to assist in finding the necessary help to regain control over her behavior. Be positive and encouraging, yet do not waiver in your belief that this person's gambling has become harmful to her and to those around her. Remember Romans 15:14: "And concerning you...I myself also am convinced that you yourselves are full of goodness, filled with all knowledge, and able also to admonish one another" (NASB). Trust in God. Trust in your gut reactions to your loved one. Speak out, if necessary.

If you are unsure about when to voice your concerns, ask God for wisdom. Be alert to vulnerable moments when the person you are concerned about is more open to hearing the truth. Observe her demeanor. Pray and wait for a time when her natural defenses are down or withdrawn. And remember, a softly whispered word of concern can be heard more clearly than a loud, intense cry of warning.

No matter if, when, or how you choose to share your concern, always continue in prayer and love. Habits do not change overnight. Insight may occur instantly, but repentance generally takes more time. Once gambling has been identified and accepted as a problem, the solution will require patience, prayer, and persistence.

If you are married to an occasional gambler, her problem is yours too. After you have identified gambling as a problem, your spouse may or may not acknowledge that a problem exists. In other words, your spouse may not be willing to work with you about her gambling. If that is the case, continue to pray for God to change your spouse's heart.

If you believe a problem exists, your goal is to assist your loved one in overcoming her gambling, not to merely vent your anger and frustration at her inappropriate behavior. Venting your frustration may be what you feel you need to do, but be wise if you do. Your spouse or friend may not be ready to hear your frustration, but God is always ready and knows how you're feeling anyway. Through prayer, ask him to provide you with an appropriate way to give voice to all of the anxiety, concern, and fear you are feeling.

Remember you are not alone in your love for the gambler. You are not alone in your concern for her. You are not alone in your desire for positive changes. Ask God for help, ask others for prayer, and be aware that professional help is available for you when the burden seems too great.

THE FREEDOM OF TRUTH

Not many of us enjoy confrontation, whether it is confronting our own hearts or confronting those of others. Instead of becoming involved in the odious task of confronting the truth, we prefer to pretend. We prefer to pretend we don't feel this way. We prefer to pretend our actions don't really cause harm. We prefer to pretend someone we care about is just fine doing what she is doing. We prefer to pretend the behavior will go away on its own.

What we really prefer is living with the lies rather than confronting the truth. It may seem easier to pretend, but that also is a lie. Sometimes we simply need to become involved, whether in evaluating our own actions or in interceding in the behavior of a loved one. It may not be easy, but it is necessary.

If gambling is adversely affecting you or someone you love, it will be a difficult problem to confront and change. If it is difficult for you to think about what it will take to change, consider what will happen if there is no change. Consider how much you are willing to exchange for the false comfort of doing nothing. Change may seem overwhelming when compared with your own ability, but what you seek is not impossible for God. We have a God who supplies our every need, whether we need courage or compassion or wisdom. Our infinite and all-powerful heavenly Father is willing to help, wanting to help, waiting to help.

HOPE FOR THE COMPULSIVE GAMBLER

At ten minutes to nine, a line had already formed outside the shed at the back of the church. Laurie hugged her sweater closer to her body to keep the wind out as she made her way across the gravel parking lot. She'd parked the car several blocks away on the off chance that someone she knew might drive by and recognize it at the neighborhood food bank. The humiliation would be too much.

As if a circle were closing in on her, Laurie was running out of options. Otherwise, she'd never have resorted to something she'd always thought was for those down on their luck. The gravel crunched under her feet as she shuffled to the back of the line. Keeping her head down, she avoided eye contact with any of the other people. She didn't want to see who they were. In no way did she want to connect with them. All she wanted was her two sacks of food. Instead of going grocery shopping three nights ago, she'd gone to the cardroom. Now the money was gone and so was her food.

Laurie was broke. No more change in the car ashtray. No more stray dollars forgotten in the pocket of a jacket. No more funds left in the checking account. No more advances on her credit cards. No more friends who hadn't already loaned her money. No more. The only thing she had plenty of was bills.

In twenty minutes she also had two sacks filled with nonperishable food items and government surplus commodities. Arms full, Laurie walked back to her car, empty and dissatisfied. What she'd gotten was food. What she needed was help.

HOPE FOR THE COMPULSIVE GAMBLER

Life can seem hopeless for someone like Laurie caught in the midst of a compulsive behavior. The past is full of broken promises made to ourselves or others. The desire to keep doing the behavior never seems to diminish long enough to give a fighting chance at breaking away in the present. The promise of the future never seems to arrive. In such a climate, despair is quick to take up residence, crowding out what little room there is for hope.

In the midst of all of that, how can we find the strength to change? The answer is, we can't. In and of ourselves, we do not have the strength to change. The most we can do is cry out for help, as the psalmist did:

> O LORD, do not rebuke me in your anger
> > or discipline me in your wrath.
> For your arrows have pierced me,
> > and your hand has come down upon me.
> Because of your wrath there is no health in my body;
> > my bones have no soundness because of my sin.
> My guilt has overwhelmed me
> > like a burden too heavy to bear....
> All my longings lie open before you, O Lord;
> > my sighing is not hidden from you....
> For I am about to fall,
> > and my pain is ever with me.
> I confess my iniquity;
> > I am troubled by my sin....

O LORD, do not forsake me;
    be not far from me, O my God.
Come quickly to help me,
    O Lord my Savior. (Psalm 38)

When all we have left is a cry for help, there is hope. When the only place left to turn is to God, there is hope. With hope, what seems like the end is really the beginning.

"I admit I am powerless over certain parts of my life and I need God's help." So states the very first step in a twelve-step program for overcoming addiction. For some, this might seem like a defeatist statement. Why begin a process for changing something as powerful as an addiction by saying we are powerless against it? Where's the hope in that?

The hope is in the second part of the admission: I need God's help. By admitting our own inability to bring about change, we cry out to God and ask him to save us. We admit we are too weak to save ourselves, and we submit our lives and our healing to him. When we do that, we are in good hands—God's hands. Admitting we are powerless allows us to abandon our own efforts at salvation and trust instead in our Savior.

When we are caught in compulsive behaviors or trying to help someone caught in compulsive behaviors, we need God's help. Only he can change our hearts and the hearts of others. Below are some practical questions and steps that God can use to offer hope when we need it most.

WORDS TO THE COMPULSIVE GAMBLER

Are you broken yet? Are you ready to admit your own powerlessness? Are you ready to admit that gambling is a problem for you? Are you ready to admit that gambling has taken control in your life?

Are you ready to say, like David, "Be pleased, O LORD, to save me; O LORD, come quickly to help me" (Psalm 40:13)?

If you have answered yes to these questions, now is not the time for despair. Now is the time for hope! With this honest appraisal of your situation, you are ready to admit you need God to rescue you. And he will!

Restoration Comes from God

The most important step you can take is to return to God. You need to admit that through gambling you have developed a relationship with an idol, a rival of God—money. This relationship with money has left you drained physically, financially, and spiritually. You have worshiped at its high places and laid down your sacrifices at its altars. It has taken everything you have of value and given you nothing in return.

Gambling has broken down your finances, maybe your employment. It has breached the strongholds of your relationships and hurt those you love most. It has destroyed your ability to feel good about yourself. This may seem like a cause for despair, not hope. God says he wants to restore you, but how can you ever be built up again?

Before you give up hope, read the book of Joel in the Old Testament. Within its pages you'll find the account of a terrible devastation, a plague of locusts consuming every green thing in sight. Has gambling made you feel like that? If your situation with gambling is not yet that bleak, it will be if you continue. Given time, gambling will consume, like locusts, every green and growing thing in your life.

Yes, the book of Joel is about devastation, but in the middle there comes a turning point, a turning of the tables, found in Joel 2:12-13: "'Even now,' declares the LORD, 'return to me with all your heart....' Rend your heart and not your garments. Return to the LORD your God, for he is gracious and compassionate, slow to anger and abounding in love." From this verse on, the tone of the book changes. The remainder of the book of Joel chronicles God's restoration of his people.

No matter the devastation gambling has brought to your life, God can restore you. He can heal you. He will heal you if you let him, if you are ready to admit your own powerlessness and your need for him.

The Power of Prayer

It is not enough for you to admit the dark side of gambling. It is not enough for you to acknowledge the pain it has caused in your life. That's a beginning, but more is required. You also need to acknowledge your inability to control your own gambling. You must cry out to God for rescue from this overwhelming compulsion. You must do as the prophet Joel recorded and rend your heart, not your garments.

Blaming gambling for the pain it has caused in your life is like rending only your garments. You must take responsibility for your own gambling behaviors and admit your inability to control them. You must get on your knees before God, bow your head, and pray for restoration. From this position, you can rend your heart. God will support you in this position, just as he has promised: "a broken and contrite heart, O God, you will not despise" (Psalm 51:17).

Through prayer, begin to reestablish the relationship with God that has been broken by your unfaithfulness with money. Through prayer, pour out your anguish and your pain over the devastation gambling has brought to your life. Through prayer, be still and listen to God's gentle answers, his quiet responses. Through prayer, restoration will begin.

Be Prepared

Gambling will not concede its power over your heart without a fight. It will try to tempt you back, seduce you with its promises, work to compromise your renewed commitment to God. It will invade your quiet moments and worm its way into your thoughts.

When the temptation comes to return to your old life of gambling, when the smooth excuses and the reasonable rationales for putting just one foot back over the line come, you must be prepared. The more gambling has taken hold of your life, the harder those behaviors will try to hang on. Don't shirk from the battle, expect it. Expect it, and be prepared.

Lift Up Your Voice

Cry out to God in prayer. Cry out to God in song. Take three or four—or more—scriptures highlighted in this book, especially meaningful to you, and memorize them. Say them silently to yourself. Shout them out loud to the world if you have to! When gambling lies to you, counter it with truth from God.

Sunday Morning, Not Saturday Night

Fighting our battles is difficult. Fighting our battles alone is nearly impossible. God has provided a supportive environment for us to recharge, renew, and recommit our lives and our hearts to him. This supportive environment is called the church.

When we get caught up and overwhelmed with activities, something has to give. Too often, that something is our regular assembly time with God's people. There are only so many hours in a day, and being able to sleep in on Sunday morning, especially after a long workweek, is tempting. We trade in spiritually energizing renewal for a few hours of physical renewal through sleep. Spiritually unsettled about where our priorities are being placed, we may even avoid church deliberately, thinking that if we avoid church we can avoid our conflicting emotions.

If gambling on Saturday night has interfered with your ability to worship on Sunday morning, it's time to return to church. It's time to gain the spiritual strength and encouragement only the body of Christ can bring you. Be open and honest with your brothers and sisters about your struggles with gambling. Gain their prayers and encouragement. There may be others in the church who have overcome similar struggles and can share with you their temptations, encourage you with their victories, and pray for you.

Turn and Run Away

There can be so much more to gambling than actually gambling. There is the atmosphere, the people, the excitement, the sights and sounds. For some of you, the gambling environment is as compelling as the gambling itself. You may be tempted to surround yourself with the environment, promising yourself that you will go but not gamble.

Perhaps your gambling is done as part of a group, and you don't want to give up the group. You say to yourself that you'll go just to be with them and you won't gamble. But you will. Accept the fact that for now and maybe forever you are not strong enough to be around gambling and not gamble. Accept it, and run away.

If being with those people is important to you, and if you are important enough to them, arrange a time and place to meet with them away from gambling. Give yourself the opportunity to explore your relationship with one another apart from gambling. You may find that gambling is what gave the relationship meaning. You may find the relationship is so meaningful, it is even better without the distraction of gambling. You may also find the others, who may not be where you are, love the gambling more than they love being with you. Be prepared for anything.

If you find you must give up those people to give up gambling, be strong enough to do so. Your first allegiance is to God, to be where God wants you to be, to do what God wants you to do. If you must give up your gambling "family," listen to what Jesus says in Luke 18:29-30: "Truly I say to you, there is no one who has left house or wife or brothers or parents or children, for the sake of the kingdom of God, who will not receive many times as much at this time and in the age to come, eternal life" (NASB). God has already arranged a family for you in the church, where your joint passion is God, not gambling. It may take time to establish new relationships or feel comfortable in a church, but God will honor your desire to obey him.

Housecleaning

Gambling has taken hold of a significant amount of time and energy in your life, to say nothing of money. As you make a commitment to refrain from gambling and refuse to enter situations where gambling is present, you may find you have time on your hands. What you do with that time could mean the difference between success and relapse.

Do you remember the parable Jesus told in the book of Luke about housecleaning? It applies to you as you "clean house" and get rid of your past gambling behaviors. "When an evil spirit comes out of a man, it goes through arid places seeking rest and does not find it. Then it says, 'I will return to the house I left.' When it arrives, it find the house swept clean and put in order. Then it goes and takes seven other spirits more wicked than itself, and they go in and live there. And the final condition of that man is worse than the first" (Luke 11:24-26).

Is cleaning house good? Yes, but it shouldn't stop there. It is not enough to merely clean house, to say to yourself, "I'm just not going to gamble." Find activities that fill up the "empty space" left from your cessation of gambling. Rediscover the joys of being with friends and family outside of a casino, away from the need to wager on which way the wind is blowing or how many steps it will take to cross the street. Again, one of the most important things you can do with your time is to reconnect with the power found in relationships with other people in God's family.

A Circle of Friends

Another excellent way to use up some of your free time is to join an accountability or support group. Accountability groups and prayer groups are available in most churches. Support groups for various struggles can also be found in church basements and extra Sunday school classrooms across the country. Ask God to direct you to a group that can support your desire for change.

An accountability group needn't be made up of other gamblers but can merely be a group of friends who are dedicated to holding each other accountable for their relationship with God. Each person in the group will have at least one area of their lives where they are battling persistent sin. For you, it may be gambling. For another, it may be anger. For another, lust. Each has a different battle, but the strategies for victory are similar. Together you can provide support and encouragement. Together you can pray with and for each other. Within the intimacy of a small group, you can feel more comfortable sharing your battles.

You may find it helpful to join an accountability group made up of others of the same gender. You may also want to consider a support group composed of those overcoming their gambling behaviors. While the group need not be made up solely of Christians, it is important to choose a group that will acknowledge your faith, your greatest weapon in this spiritual battle. It will be of limited value if your faith, your greatest asset, is not allowed to be discussed and supported.

In a small group you may have an opportunity to give glory to God in your struggle with gambling in view of those who don't know the Lord; this can be a tremendous motivation for you to change. You may not care what others think of you, but you do care deeply how others view God. As a child of God, how you approach and deal with the struggle you are undergoing can be a tremendous witness to the power of your heavenly Father.

Your local phone book is a tremendous resource for finding support groups. Twelve-step groups like Gamblers Anonymous are listed in the phone books of most major cities. To find out about a group meeting in your area, you can contact Gamblers Anonymous at P.O. Box 17173, Los Angeles, CA 90017, or call them at (213) 386-8789. The Gamblers Helpline at 1-800-994-0899 is also a good resource. You can also contact the National Gambling Council Helpline, which provides information and referrals to Gamblers Anonymous groups and to counselors who specialize in gambling problems. Their toll-free phone number is 1-800-522-4700.

Even if there is no support group meeting in your community, you can access groups over the Internet. Besides Web sites for Gamblers Anonymous, there are also home pages devoted to Christian topics where you can be encouraged and prayed for by believers from all over the country, like crosswalk.com. Be aware, however, of the pitfalls involved with the Internet. Not everyone is who he says he is on the World Wide Web. Caution and discretion are valuable shields when surfing the Net.

Gambling, while a powerful compulsion, is not unlike many addictive behaviors people fall prey to. If there is no group meeting in your area specifically dealing with gambling, consider joining a support group for other addictions such as eating disorders, chemical dependency, or sexual addictions. You may find the behavior different, but the reasons behind the behavior are strikingly similar. The behaviors will be different, but the path to restoration is the same: through the grace of God, the power of the Spirit, and the redemption of Jesus Christ.

There are also many godly professionals—counselors and therapists—who will be able to assist you in overcoming the pull to gamble. Together you can explore your reasons for gambling and work as a team to bring control and sanity back into your life. Gambling isn't a problem that needs to stay hidden. Help is out there. Be persistent until you find it.

Give Up Control

Until you have recovered the necessary self-control over money, you may want to consider having someone else handle your financial affairs. This other person could be a spouse, another family member, an attorney, or a financial advisor. This is not a step to be taken lightly. Your spouse or another family member handling your money could become a source of contention and friction between you. If it is an attorney or an accountant, you will have legal papers to sign and honor. Though drastic, giving up control of your money to another person can provide an immediate, daily reminder of both your precarious position and of your desire to gain control of your life again.

Another way to cede control of your money, without taking this drastic step, is to seek out the local Consumer Credit Counseling Service in your area. This service is staffed by volunteers who assist those with financial difficulties stemming from a variety of issues, including gambling. Together you can assess your financial situation and come up with a strategy for restoring your credit and putting you back on a firm financial footing. Gambling may have left your finances in shambles. As long as this situation is allowed to persist, you will feel the pressure to "correct" it the way you've tried in the past, through gambling. Having a concrete plan to restore your finances can help keep you focused on the biblical steps of patient, steady, and prudent compiling of assets to repair and rebuild your financial situation.

Twenty-Twenty Vision

Gambling does not want you to see the truth. Instead it wants to weave a distorted picture of fun, excitement, fortune, and fame. For a while it will be very tempting to take your eyes off God and cast wistful looks at gambling. Remember what happened when Peter took his eyes off Jesus? He sank like a stone in the water. You will sink back into gambling if you take your eyes off of God.

Keep your eyes fixed on God and revel in all of his truths. Yes, you have gambled, but God has forgiven you. Yes, you have wasted money and time, but God will restore them. Yes, you gave up things of value for worthless things, but you have returned to the Lord and are now seeking his presence, the most valuable thing of all.

If there is one thing God does not want you to lose sight of in this journey away from gambling, it is hope. Hope means there will come a day when you have no time for even a stray thought about gambling. Hope means there will come a day when you are able to pay your bills again and restore your credit. Hope means there will come a day when your spouse won't question where you've been if you come home late. Hope means there will come a day when your children's memory of this time in their lives—when you loved gambling more than them—will fade and be replaced by vivid thoughts of your care and concern. Hope means there is a tomorrow out there for you. Hope is the steadfast love of the Lord that never ceases. Hope is his unending mercy, new every morning.

Then you will be like David in Psalm 40:1-3 and say, "I waited patiently for the LORD; he turned to me and heard my cry. He lifted me out of the slimy pit, out of the mud and mire; he set my feet on a rock and gave me a firm place to stand. He put a new song in my mouth, a hymn of praise to our God. Many will see and fear and put their trust in the LORD."

WORDS TO A FRIEND OR LOVED ONE

If hope is important to the compulsive gambler, it may be even more important to you. You may be the only one to cradle hope until he is able to reclaim it. You must ask yourself if you are strong enough to keep that hope alive. It will not be easy.

It will not be easy to watch as someone you love falls flat on his face, gets up, and falls again. It will not be easy to step back and allow your loved one to experience the painful consequences of his actions. It will not be easy to hear, over and over again, your loved one's empty promises to change before he turns around and betrays his words. It will not be easy to love the gambler when all of that person's love is devoted to the very thing that is destroying him.

God knows it won't be easy. "If you love those who love you, what credit is that to you? Even 'sinners' love those who love them. And if you do good to those who are good to you, what credit is that to you? Even 'sinners' do that.... Be merciful, just as your Father is merciful" (Luke 6:32-33,36). It won't be easy to love and help a compulsive gambler, but if you won't, who will?

Do No Harm

At this point, it is important to differentiate between what would be helpful and what would be harmful as you deal with the compulsive gambler.

As you relate to your loved one who is addicted to gambling, it would be harmful to

- choose to do or say nothing to the compulsive gambler in order to preserve the relationship
- lend the compulsive gambler money in order to help him win
- accompany the gambler in order to monitor his gambling
- become bitter and angry about his gambling
- trust only in the gambler's ability to change

It would be helpful to

- pray daily for yourself and for the gambler
- find a caring friend in whom you can confide and seek guidance and strength
- clearly communicate your love to the gambler as well as your personal boundaries regarding his gambling
- find out all you can about gambling support groups in your area
- trust more in God than in your relationship with the gambler

Gam-Anon, a nationwide support group for those whose spouse, loved one, or family member has a gambling problem, can be a source of help as you differentiate between what is helpful and harmful to your friend. You can contact Gam-Anon at P.O. Box 157, Whitestone, NY 11357 or by phone at (718) 352-1671.

When It's Time to Go

If the gambler you are concerned about is a friend, your ability to influence his behavior may not be enough to make him change. Simply put, he may value gambling more than your friendship. Naturally, you will want to do whatever you can to convince him to change. It may not be enough. There may come a time when you need to withdraw yourself from the friendship rather than to continue in it and support your friend's self-destructive behavior. A relationship with your friend is only possible if he places enough value in it to maintain it. A time may come when you have said all you can say, done all you can do. If that time comes, your relationship with your friend ends, but your care and concern need not. Through constant prayer and petition, lift up his plight to God and ask for his deliverance. Trust in God to change hearts and provide an opportunity for reconciliation.

If a family member is a compulsive gambler, your bonds can be more tightly wound than those of friendship. If your spouse is a compulsive gambler, the devotion that rightly belongs to you is being diverted to an impersonal activity. If your parent is a compulsive gambler, the nurture that rightly belongs to you is absent. If a sibling is a compulsive gambler, the familial relationship that rightly belongs to you is being cast aside for strangers. You love that person; he is part of you. When he hurts himself, you are injured also. What should be your response?

Your only response is to love. Love may mean rebuking and admonishing him for the behavior that is hurting him so much. Accept no excuses from him. Gently remind him of the truth. And sometimes hardest of all, refuse to assist him in his gambling. In the midst of all this, pray.

There may come a time when you will need to refuse to be a party to his self-destruction. For your own safety and sanity, you may need to refuse to continue to live with the gambler in his life as a compulsive gambler. You may need to offer him a choice between love of gambling and love of you.

KEEPING HOPE ALIVE

Our compulsive sins and addictive behaviors are almost like demons at times, inhabiting our minds and will, tormenting us and attempting to tear us apart. Jesus told his disciples that some demons could only be removed by prayer. The demon of compulsive gambling seems to be immune to the remedies of common man. It cannot be cajoled and seems resistant to persuasion. This demon requires an encounter with Jesus.

If you are fighting the demon of compulsive gambling, only Jesus can save you. Only his power is stronger than your compulsion to gamble. Only hope in him is powerful enough to override the hopelessness of your addiction. The time to cry out to him is now. The time to admit your powerlessness is now. The time to turn the struggle over to him is today.

If someone you love is fighting this demon called compulsive gambling, your love won't be enough to save him. Your conviction in the destructive nature of that person's behavior won't be enough to convince him to stop. Only God's truth is powerful enough to break through that person's delusion. Pray without ceasing. Draw yourself closer and closer to God. Let the witness of your life shine through the darkness of your friend's addiction. Keep hoping. Keep praying. Keep believing. Keep trusting. Keep loving.

May the hope for restoration and a new beginning be a living testimony to the grace of God.

14

HOPE FOR THE
TEENAGE GAMBLER

Look, I don't have it." Jack tried to keep his voice down, but desperation increased the volume of his whisper.

"Well, this isn't enough! When are ya gonna get me the rest?" Randall, on the other hand, couldn't care less about keeping his voice down. All he wanted was his money.

"I get paid on Friday. I can get the rest to you then," Jack replied, thinking rapidly to himself how his paycheck was going to stretch that far. He needed to pay his folks for his car payment, fill the tank with gas, pay Randall, and still have enough money left over to last for two weeks. This whole thing had gotten out of hand way too fast.

For a while there, the ride had been great. With his friends egging him on, he'd made some outrageous bets on the outcome of some *Monday Night Football* games and had actually won. The more he won, the more he kept betting. The more he bet, the more he began to lose. He'd lost quite a bit to Randall.

"Friday, huh?" Randall asked, clearly unhappy. "Well, I'll see you on Friday, and you better have the rest of it." He looked Jack square in the eyes with a no-nonsense expression, turned, and strode down the hallway. Jack let out his breath and watched him walk away.

Down the hall, near the entrance to the gym, Jack noticed Ashley coming his way. She glanced up about that time and their eyes met. Ashley's eyes got very big, right before she ducked quickly into the double doors to the gym.

"Wait!" Jack yelled, running into the gym and catching up to her. "Ashley, I really need that money you owe me."

She refused to turn around and continued walking at a fast pace across the gym floor. "Look," she said in a strident whisper, "I don't have it."

A TIME OF RENEWAL

As we've already discussed in earlier chapters, one of the populations most at-risk for gambling behaviors is the young. Flush with emerging needs, they often lack the maturity of experience to discern appropriate ways for filling those needs. Impatient, they seek instant gratification and thrills. Independent, they seek to declare their release from restraint by engaging in adult behaviors. One of the adult behaviors they are engaging in and expanding upon is gambling.

Gambling fills many needs at once. It is stimulating, gratifying, adult. Adolescents are on the verge of adulthood and eager to make adult choices. This is a particularly vulnerable time. In 2 Timothy 2:22, Paul sends out this admonition to young people: "Flee the evil desires of youth, and pursue righteousness, faith, love and peace, along with those who call on the Lord out of a pure heart." Unfortunately, if you stop and ask teenagers on the street what they are pursuing, how many of them would answer righteousness, faith, love, or peace? The maturity of faith often appears inconsistent with the independence of adulthood. To teens, faith often seems to belong to the realm of small children and old people, not emerging adults.

Teenagers may seek to engage in behaviors that declare their independence from adults, but they too often seek adult behaviors to do so. Declaring their adulthood, they emulate what they see adults doing around them. As more teens see adults gambling, more teens will, in turn, gamble. When they do, they are ensnared at an even greater rate than adults. This is a cycle with chilling ramifications.

God did not make a mistake when he programmed adolescence. It is a time of great awakening. It is a time of endless optimism and possibilities. It is a time of renewal. Why would a generation need renewal? To answer that question, one needs to look no farther than the Old Testament. The Israelites were constantly falling away from God, and God often relied on new generations to bring hope and turn again to him. When Moses and the Israelites left Egypt, in fact, they had to wander in the desert until forty years had passed and a new generation was born. The new generation turned from the sins of the old, sought God, and entered the Promised Land God had waiting for them.

Young people have the opportunity to turn the tables on gambling and refuse to be caught up in the behaviors that ensnare them. They can declare their autonomy from the world, give their allegiance to God, and gain freedom in Christ. Just as teens have great potential to fall into the gambling trap, they have great potential to get out of it. In a culture hostile to God, spirituality can be the ultimate statement of independence.

WORDS TO THE YOUTHFUL GAMBLER

It may seem to you that adults are a rather negative group of people. We dwell on what might happen in any given situation and assume the worst. We constantly advise you about dangers that never seem to materialize. We fail to acknowledge your experience or intelligence. At least that's how it might seem to you.

When we see you making a bet on a basketball game, we panic and assume you've got the number of a bookie taped inside your locker. We lecture you on the evils of wagering and make dire predictions about losing more than you win. We spout platitudes like, "The advantage always goes to the house." We assume you're not smart enough to be able to make an intelligent bet. We talk about lost money, bad people, the burden of debt, traveling down the wrong path. At least that's how it might seem to you.

As frustrating as all of those dire predictions may seem, what's even more frustrating is how often they're true. We know they're true because we've seen them happen in our own lives and the lives of others. It's not that we're better or smarter than you are. It's just that we've made mistakes and see the chance for you to avoid those mistakes and the pain they cause.

Basically, we're scared. We're scared you're going to make those same mistakes. We're scared you're going to make worse ones. We're scared that you won't listen to us and you'll do damage to yourself. We're scared we're somehow to blame. More than anything else, we just want you to listen, really listen, to our warnings and take them to heart:

Gambling can be an addictive behavior. Like getting caught in a strong riptide, gambling can pull you out into deep water more quickly than you can possibly imagine. It traps adults, sure, but it's trapping people your age at two to two and a half times the rate of adults.

We have failed you. We have allowed gambling to overwhelm this society we've given you. Our cowardice and apathy have placed you at risk for behaviors that can ruin your life. Because we have failed you, it is vital that you not fail yourself. Be alert to the traps we have fallen into and avoid them. Be smarter than we were.

Some things are stronger than any of us. As a young person, you are on the cusp of the rest of your life. Your possibilities and potential stretch out before you like an open road. When adults put up roadblocks or warning signs along that road, you don't particularly like that. But being older, we've been down the road before. We know where that side road ends up, and we don't want you to experience what it's like to travel that road. The forces along that road are stronger than you are. We know because they have overpowered us before.

Maybe there are adults in your life who are still on those side roads. Maybe you don't hear warnings about gambling because your parents gamble themselves. Take a hard look at their lives, at their relationships. Is it worth it? Do they seem in control of their gambling or does their gambling seem to control them? Are you willing to lose as they have just to keep going down that road?

Gambling is not a sign of manhood. Becoming sucked into the lies of a compulsive behavior is no way to show you are an adult. In our culture, teenagers who embrace gambling are predominantly older adolescent males. You are using gambling as a way to announce your adulthood to the world, your friends, your parents. But being an adult is more than manipulating friends to bet with you. Being an adult is more than seeking out your self-esteem through winning a game of chance. Being an adult is more than the ability to predict the outcome of a sporting event.

When you started, you may have thought that gambling was about being an adult. Accepting and embracing the risk may have seemed like a good way to show what you're made of. Knowing how to win, however, is not the measure of adulthood. Winning is easy; the hard part is losing. Now, as you seek to control your gambling, you have a real opportunity to experience what being an adult is all about. Being an adult is accepting responsibility for your actions. Being an adult is knowing when you're in over your head and asking for help. Being an adult is finding the courage to examine your life and make necessary changes. Being an adult is having the strength to do something extremely difficult because it is the right thing to do.

Stop gambling not because we tell you to but because you know it's right. Your life is just beginning, full of promise and dreams. Gambling promises you a way to fulfill your dreams, but all it ultimately will do is suck you dry. It will rob you of promise and leave you with nothing. Be smarter and stronger than we were, recognize its lies, and resist its pull.

Part of resisting gambling's pull is knowing how to handle peer pressure. What do you say when your friends want to gamble and you know you shouldn't? Do you tell them the truth? Do you lie and pretend you have something else to do? Do you go anyway but just promise yourself you won't gamble? Do you endanger yourself for the sake of your friends? The best answer to each of the last three questions is no. It is best to tell your friends the truth.

Telling the truth, of course, is risky. To help convince you to take that risk, ask yourself another question: If your friends understand the danger gambling is to you and still expect you to gamble, are they really your friends?

Peer pressure is a fact of life for teenagers. Someone from the crowd will expect you to do something you shouldn't. Whether it is gambling, sex, drugs, stealing, or something else, a time will come when you will have to stand up for yourself. Your parents won't be there to do it for you. Other friends won't step forward to support you. The one who will have to take a stand for what is best for you is you.

It can be lonely doing the right thing, but you will not be alone. God fully supports your choice to do what is right for yourself. Saying no to your friends is often the same thing as saying yes to God. If the choice comes down to pleasing your friends or pleasing God, choose God. Ask him to strengthen your resolve and provide you with the wisdom needed to present your reasons to your friends. If they truly are your friends, they will understand. If they are not your friends, it's better to know that now. Ask God to provide you with the kind of friends who will look out for what is best for you and support you. Those friends are out there, and God knows just who they are.

There is another reason to tell your friends the truth: They may need to hear it for themselves. You may be the only person with the courage to tell the rest of your friends when something they want to do is a bad idea. If it's a bad idea for you, it's probably a bad idea for them. A final question: Do you care enough about your friends to tell them the truth?

Explaining your reasons for not wanting to gamble can provide an excellent opportunity for taking your friendships to a deeper level—a level with greater immunity to peer pressure, a level where honesty is presented in love and where friends watch out for the good of each other, a level where the hope you have in a loving God is accepted as part of who you are. Such friendships are rare and worth fighting for. Keep looking. Keep praying.

Remember you have people around you who want to help. If you find yourself in the midst of a gambling compulsion that has overtaken you, ask for help. Ask your parents. If they cannot or will not help you, ask another adult. Ask a teacher, a school counselor, a mentor, the parent of a friend. Ask a coach, a pastor, a youth minister, a coworker. Seek help for yourself. Our fear for you may weaken our ability to really hear and see your truth. Be stubborn and demand we listen to you.

More than anything, remember that God knows your name. He knows the number of hairs on your head. He knows when you come and when you go. You are important to him. Your life, your dreams are part of a cosmic plan. He wants you to follow his steps above all others, above even the steps of the adults around you. This is his promise to you: "Do not let your heart envy sinners, but always be zealous for the fear of the LORD. There is surely a future hope for you, and your hope will not be cut off" (Proverbs 23:17-18).

You can hide from your parents, you can even hide from yourself, but you can't hide from God. No matter how fast you move, no matter how clever your excuses, no matter how hard you try to keep it under cover or under control—God knows. He cannot be fooled or distracted. He knows of your gambling and holds you accountable for it. He knows and wants you to stop because he has better things in store for you.

You can make gambling a thing of the past. It may seem as if you constantly live in the here and now. The future is the job you need to go to tomorrow or the test you have to take next week. Waiting is torture, and a month's time seems an eternity. A year is so far away, it hardly seems real. Within these feelings, your gambling problem casts an enormous shadow, dwarfing any hope for change. Remain optimistic. Work through your compulsion one day at a time. Find courage from God for today, and don't worry about tomorrow. It's okay to admit that it can be tough just making it through today. Jesus tells us in Matthew 6:34, "Do not worry about tomorrow, for tomorrow will worry about itself. Each day has enough trouble of its own."

Because you have gambled once doesn't mean you need to gamble again. It is so easy to get into a pattern, a predictable way of reacting to life. You figure if you've done it once, you'll do it again. If you've done it twice, you'll do it forever. This simply isn't true, especially because you are young.

One of the wonderful things about your age is the room for second chances. You're starting over all the time. You're starting over in new grades. You're starting over in new relationships. You're starting over physically as you grow and mature. So start over where gambling is concerned. Outgrow it and move on.

If you are gambling, you need to think about why. Ask yourself what gambling does for you, how it makes you feel, how it makes other people feel about you. If you have developed a compulsive gambling habit, you have been using gambling as a way to relate to your life and to others. What is gambling covering up? What is it compensating for? What hole are you trying to fill?

There are other and better ways to fill that hole than gambling. Gambling will only cause you to sink into a deeper hole than the one you are trying to fill. Gambling is not the way out. Gambling may be fun, but that fun is the gaping maw at the edge of the abyss.

WORDS TO PARENTS

From reading this book you now know your son's or daughter's gambling is not a harmless activity. Even if she is not presently gambling excessively, the potential for out-of-control behavior is real. You need to be alert and aware of the state of mind of your teenager.

As with other addictive behaviors, there are signs that may tell you something is wrong with your teen:

Inappropriate ways of declaring adulthood. Gambling is a way for a teen, especially a teenage boy, to announce his independence to the world. It will probably not be the only form of announcement your teen will make. Be alert for other ways your teenager is declaring her independence from you, especially inappropriate or harmful ways. She may decide to cease following family rules. If she does continue to follow your rules, it may be done begrudgingly or in a hostile manner. Especially watch how well your teen follows your rules for returning to the family home at night. If she is staying out late, find out where and why.

Excessive wagering with family and friends. Adolescent gambling most often begins with people the teenager knows. Be alert for wagering between your teen and her friends. Be aware if side bets are a component of games being played or games being watched on television. Further, evaluate your own behavior around your teenager to ascertain whether your behavior might be contributing to your teen's desire to gamble. If you gamble, she will be more likely to gamble also.

An unexplainable increase or decrease in money. If your teen is in the midst of the winning phase in gambling, she may suddenly have a great deal of money and no explanation for it. Don't expect your teen to brag about her winnings to you though. Observe your teen's purchases or spending habits. Are new clothes showing up? What about gifts to friends or a date? If your teen is in the midst of the losing phase, she may suddenly have a dramatic loss of funds. Has your teen begun to ask you for cash for small purchases, like food, gas, movies, or video games? Are these items your teen previously paid for? Be alert to how much money your teen has, either more or less.

Changes in attitudes about work. The teenagers who have jobs and disposable income are most at risk for compulsive gambling. Watch for a sudden decrease in desire to work and/or a sudden increase in the amount of time spent working. If your teen is winning money through gambling, she may decide work is unnecessary. If your teen is losing money through gambling, she may desperately seek to work longer hours in order to pay off gambling debts or acquire additional gambling funds.

Unexplained loss of your own money. When your gambling teen inevitably begins to experience the losing phase, she may steal money from you to pay off gambling debts or to continue to gamble. As terrible as it may sound, be alert to the money you have available and if amounts of it are missing without explanation.

Mood swings and personality changes. This can be difficult, given the built-in mood swings of teenagers. You have to really know your teen to be able to distinguish between her normal fluctuations and those drastic ups and downs, possibly fueled by her gambling activity. Winning will produce euphoria and losing will produce despair or anger. If your teen exhibits this up-and-down pattern, a red flag should go up in your mind. It might be gambling, or it might be something else. Either way, you need to know!

Other addictions. Teenage gambling has been linked to smoking, drugs, and alcohol. If one is present, the other may also be a factor. It may be that your teen began gambling as a secondary activity, linked to smoking, drugs, or alcohol. Given its compulsive nature, gambling may now be as significant or more as those other behaviors. Don't assume that because you've uncovered one behavior you've uncovered them all. Be courageous and keep looking.

Increased isolation from family, friends, or usual activities. Gambling takes time as well as money. If your teen is gambling, she will need to find a place to do it. She will often need to find people to gamble with or against. To do this, time spent with family or established friends may decrease. Activities your teen used to engage in may be abandoned in favor of unspecified, vague explanations of going out or being with friends. If your teen is drawing away from you, be sure to investigate what is taking your place.

What You Can Do to Help

If your teenager has developed a gambling addiction, you have a choice in how you respond to her. No matter what choice you make, you should respond in love. This doesn't mean you overlook what she is doing. Instead, responding to your teen's gambling addiction in love means you commit to placing her needs above your own. This is the essence of love.

As you respond in love, your teen may need you to

- establish boundaries she will fight against
- set limits on her activities
- care enough to confront her on the truth of her activities
- admit your own culpability in her gambling problem
- love her more than you love her privacy
- take the lead in providing the help she needs
- provide guidance in her access to friends
- financially commit to getting any professional help necessary
- pay her debt
- forgive her

Consider taking the following steps if you discover your teen is gambling to excess:

Increase your presence in her life and activities. If your teen is gambling regularly or compulsively, she needs your help and guidance to stop. She also needs your presence to act as a barrier to her ability to gamble in secret. Until your teen overcomes this behavior, you as the parent may need to reinsert yourself into her life for the purpose of active supervision. Your teen will probably howl, but do not be dissuaded. Explain that your increased oversight is necessary until she has demonstrated obedience by ceasing to gamble and has reestablished your trust.

Establish rules and guidelines regarding what activities are permitted and which are not. Inform your teen of your accepted activities and outline the consequences of engaging in unacceptable activities. Be prepared to back up your words and carry out those consequences. Be prepared also to expend effort in monitoring your teen's activities.

Don't make your teen's gambling a family secret. Confide in members of your church and enlist their aid through prayer. Talk to the school counselor or a professional therapist. It is not necessary to expose your teen to shame through an indiscriminate disclosure of her struggle, but relieve the pressure of discovery by informing others who can either help or simply need to know. Encourage your teen to talk to other teens or trusted adults about her desire to stop gambling. Secrets are powerful. Don't let that power work against you or your teen.

Trust in God's power. Pray for your teen. Confess your shortcomings to her, and ask for forgiveness. Commit to assisting your teen in whatever way necessary to cease gambling and to heal damages from gambling.

These steps will not be easy, but they may very well save your teen. Adolescence takes it toll on the self-esteem and natural optimism of teenagers. So much around them and in them is changing, they can have a difficult time keeping up. They can feel awkward, out of place, ugly, lonely, unappreciated, misunderstood. They can feel pressured, stressed out, unable to cope with life. Tragically, some teens find living this way a burden too great to bear. They adopt glaringly self-destructive behaviors, from promiscuous sexual activity to reckless driving to substance abuse to suicide. Teens are naturally buoyant, but the strain of gambling can tip the scales into the realm of despondency. Simply put, gambling could break your teen. Fight for your teen by fighting your own desire to give in and feel better for the moment. Be firm in love.

Healing Power

We are called to project hope into the darkened corners of this world. As adults, we do this through the knowledge of our experiences with God in the past. As teens, we do this through the unquenchable spirit of youth. Whether adult or teen, we do this through the power of God. United in God, barriers of age can be broken down. The fact of the matter is we need each other. Teens need adults for the wisdom they have from their life experiences. Adults need teens for the enthusiasm they have from their purity and promise.

Gambling does not need to be a source of contention between teens and adults, between parents and children. If gambling has influenced your family, you will need to be united, rather than separate, to combat its forces. Draw together, to God and to each other. Be gentle and compassionate with each other. Listen, really listen, to each other as you seek healing for yourself and those you love.

15

THE SOURCE OF HOPE

Head bowed and hands raised, Caleb let the last few words of the song penetrate his being. "Thank you, Lord," he sang softly, both the ending phrase of the song and a prayer of heartfelt gratitude. While the band continued to play quietly in the background, Caleb thought back over the past year. Overwhelming gratefulness was the only response possible. In the past year, God had woven back together the torn threads of his life.

A lump in his throat formed every time Caleb thought about how close he'd come to losing it all: his faith, his family, his home, his job. He'd almost lost it trying to get just a little bit more than he already had, as if all of that wasn't enough. Caleb kept shoveling in more and more of the valuable things in his life into the pit of gambling, a void that refused to be filled. Soon he ceased to recognize what he was shoveling, totally caught up in the mere act of shoveling for all he was worth.

With clarity he remembered the day his clouded mind cleared. Molly's despair had blown in like a strong wind, exposing every excuse for his gambling. Tears streaming down her face, red from anger, frustration, and sadness, she had delivered her ultimatum: Stop gambling or lose her. Even if she stayed, she warned him, he'd still lose her. His gambling was eating her up inside until soon there wouldn't be anything left.

It was the hardest thing he'd ever done, to admit to his wife he wasn't strong enough to stop. She'd just smiled then, as if the sun had come out all of a sudden, and hugged him harder than he could remember. It was okay if he wasn't strong enough, she told him, because God was. God was able if Caleb was willing.

GOD IS THE SOURCE

The past twenty years have shown how popular gambling can be. True, the gambling industry has targeted the American population in a shrewd, effective way. However, no matter how shrewd the advertising, the industry could not have been as effective if there had not been a latent demand for gambling. If people like Caleb were not truly interested in what gambling had to offer, no amount of advertising would have been able to convince them to spend so much time, money, and energy on gambling.

Gambling has existed over different times and within different cultures because human needs have existed over different times and cultures. The current sales approach to gambling may be flashy and sophisticated, but the needs gambling promises to meet are fundamental.

Needs are not wrong. They exist. They have influence in our lives. It is futile to refuse to recognize them. Consciously or unconsciously, we seek to fill the needs we have.

Ultimately, the place for fulfillment of needs lies at the source of those needs—God. God created us with voids to be filled to bring us into a deepening relationship with him. This is not done out of spite, but out of love. Since God is the creator of the void, he alone is able to fill it. One of our deepest needs is the need for relationship. In God's design, others can fill that need to a certain extent, but only he can fill it completely. As we seek ways to fill up our voids, we are really seeking God. When we choose him to fill the voids within us, we come to understand him better.

God does not hide from us, as if playing some cosmic game of hide-

and-seek. As Paul writes, "For since the creation of the world God's invisible qualities—his eternal power and divine nature—have been clearly seen, being understood from what has been made, so that men are without excuse" (Romans 1:20). Jeremiah 29:13-14 puts it this way: "'You will seek me and find me when you seek me with all your heart. I will be found by you,' declares the LORD."

Our seeking is designed to lead us closer to God. Sin, however, detours our search, drawing us away from God. Gambling in and of itself is not a sin. We sin when we love gambling or any activity more than God. The activity becomes our idol, and we give our love and devotion to it instead of to God. When we turn to gambling to fill up the needs in our lives, we sin against God by trusting in a man-made activity to save us. Gambling in this context brings nothing but pain, misery, and unfulfilled needs.

Why should we settle for less than what God intended for us? If we acknowledge the voids he has made in our lives and seek him to fill those voids, our lives are complete and our relationship with God grows. What can we learn then about ourselves and about God through the needs gambling tries to fill?

GAMBLING FOR THRILLS

Many gamblers are thrill seekers. At the moment of the big win, the gambler feels empowered, invincible, set apart from the mundane rules of the here and now. Winning is intoxicating—a heady swirl of amazement, relief, exaltation, being special. This potent mixture of the big win hooks the gambler into his gambling behavior as he seeks to recreate, over and over again, that amazing feeling.

Thrill seekers yearn to soar above the routine. Gambling fills their need for transcendence. God understands this need and has devised an incredible way to experience all of those feelings. By comparison, gambling is a poor substitute. How has God provided for transcendence? Through the awesome experience of worshiping him. Glory, not gambling, is the way to achieve true transcendence.

After the prayerful interlude of the song, the band began to increase their volume, carrying the congregation along on the rising tide of their music. As the crescendo of the song merged with his own intense feelings of thanksgiving, Caleb felt transported into the presence of God. The experience was so heady, he wanted to laugh and weep at the same time. With certainty, Caleb realized this was what he was created for. Every other thrill was a cheap imitation compared with communing with the God of the universe.

The sense of thrill has a definite pattern. First, danger, or risk, generates fear. Next we decide to undertake the activity regardless of the risk and fear. Finally, we see the outcome of that decision. If we win, we feel an overwhelming sense of relief and fear is replaced with exaltation. This relief is the thrill some of us yearn for.

Choosing to trust an awesome, transcendent God could be viewed as a gamble. First, we start with fear. The Bible says that fear, properly placed, is good. "The fear of the LORD," Psalm 111:10 says, "is the beginning of wisdom." Proverbs 9:10 echoes this thought: "The fear of the LORD is the beginning of wisdom, and knowledge of the Holy One is understanding." As we draw closer to God in worship to him, we come to understand his awesome nature and divine power. We come face to face with his glory. This can be a fearful experience. "I saw the Lord seated on a throne, high and exalted, and the train of his robe filled the temple.... And they were calling to one another: 'Holy, holy, holy is the LORD Almighty; the whole earth is full of his glory'" (Isaiah 6:1,3). What was Isaiah's response to this experience of worship? Fear. "Woe to me!... I am ruined!" he cries out (Isaiah 6:5). When we truly come to understand who we are and who God is, we have every reason to fear.

Fear is the beginning place in a relationship with God, but it was never meant as the ending place. Our loving Father has much more in mind. First John 4:18 reminds us, "There is no fear in love. But perfect love drives out fear." After we realize the risk involved in being in the presence of an omnipotent deity, we take our biggest gamble—faith. We have faith in a loving Father and gamble on his mercy and grace. We trust him to see our lives, our brokenness, and our dirtiness and still love us and want to make us clean.

The outcome of this gamble brings relief and exaltation: Christ has already secured the victory for us. We are winners. When we gamble on God, we win forgiveness and a relationship with him. To put it in the language of gambling, each of us "hit the jackpot" when Christ died for us on the cross. Christ conquered sin and death so we can say, "Thanks be to God! He gives us the victory through our Lord Jesus Christ" (1 Corinthians 15:57). In worship to God we remember that victory. Salvation and eternal life are the jackpot through Christ. No earthly win will ever top that. The rules of sin and death no longer apply to us. We have transcended them through Christ. And because it is a victory that never fades, we can experience it in worship every day.

What could be more thrilling than a transcendent worship experience, praising the awesome God of the universe? Shortchanging our need for transcendence by settling for the outcome of a man-made game of chance is pathetic. God has so much more for us. If it is thrill a person needs, God is more than able to provide. Transfer your need for thrill from gambling to God and be amazed.

What we need tells us who we are. What we need also tells us who God is. If he placed the need within us, it must be for a purpose. Why would God place within us a need for transcendence? Because without it we would settle only for ourselves and would not seek him. We would forever remain earthbound when all along God has created us for heaven.

Practical Steps

If gambling has awakened a need for transcendence in you, accept this need but reject the way you have been filling it. One way to turn to God instead of gambling is to get involved in a church. Churches meet in every city and town across this country. Some meet on Sunday mornings, some on Sunday nights, some on Saturday nights. Some have loud bands praising God with a steady beat. Some have choirs of human voices softly singing praises to God. Find a church that you feel comfortable in and called to and experience true worship.

Don't be disheartened if it takes awhile for you to begin to feel like worshiping. You've been numbing your need for transcendence through the artificial high of gambling. By comparison, a worship or praise time in church may seem tame. Don't be confused. Gambling—with its intense experience of sights, sounds, smells, and adrenaline—is all about the outside affecting the inside; it's about the energy of the outside covering up the emptiness on the inside.

Worship is the opposite. Worship is about allowing God's Spirit in you to radiate outward as you meditate through song and praise on the enormity of God's love and power. As your spirit connects with God's Spirit, worship expands you outward.

Give yourself a chance. Give God a chance. Allow him to lead you to a place where you can experience him through worship.

There are ways you can prepare yourself for worship before you ever step inside a church building. Try any or all of the following to help enhance your experience of worship:

- Wake up a half-hour or hour early and get away by yourself before you go to church. Take a walk or find a quiet corner where you live and meditate on the nature of God.
- Take your Bible and spend some time in prayer, asking God to give insight as you open up the Scriptures. Pray for his Spirit to fill you with a desire to experience true worship.

- During your travel to church, listen to music of worship and praise on the radio or through a tape or CD. Sing along with the music wholeheartedly.
- Pray before you enter the church that God will protect your heart from distraction and allow you to experience him through the worship.

As you begin this new phase of your journey with God, commit your heart to him, pledging to be honest with him always about what you feel, what you think, what you need. No matter what.

GAMBLING FOR MONEY

The Bible says that money is the root of all evil, right? So having a need for money is a sin, correct? No. Actually, the Bible says that it is the *love* of money that is at the root of all kinds of evil (1 Timothy 6:10). It is not the need for money that gets us into trouble. God understands our need for money as a way to provide for our physical requirements. In our culture, this is done through money, just as it was in Jesus' day.

The Pharisees sought to trick Jesus by asking whether they should pay taxes to Rome. Jesus answered by saying: "'Bring me a denarius and let me look at it.' They brought the coin, and he asked them, 'Whose portrait is this? And whose inscription?' 'Caesar's,' they replied. Then Jesus said to them, 'Give to Caesar what is Caesar's and to God what is God's'" (Mark 12:15-17). Money, even a denarius with an inscription of an ungodly Roman emperor, has value. The difficulty is in knowing what that value is.

Consider the following verse from James: "Now listen, you who say, 'Today or tomorrow we will go to this or that city, spend a year there, carry on business and make money.' Why, you do not even know what will happen tomorrow. What is your life? You are a mist that appears for a little while and then vanishes. Instead, you ought to say, 'If it is the Lord's will, we will live and do this or that'" (James 4:13-15). What is the sin here? Is it in desiring to make money? No, it is in desiring to do any-thing without recognizing the sovereignty of God in all of our decisions.

Caleb looked over at Molly and saw the faint smile on her face as the collection basket passed by. He rolled his eyes in acknowledgment of her grin and smiled back. It felt great to put their contribution in the basket. Not because of the amount, certainly, but because he was able to let go of the money at all. A year earlier, he'd found a reason every Sunday to avoid par-ticipating in the contribution: He didn't like the way the money was used. They had too many bills to pay. He'd forgotten to bring the checkbook and he didn't want to put in cash. The truth was, he had other plans for the money and had no intention of wasting it on God.

When people consume their lives with gambling as a way to attain wealth, they are putting faith in money that they should be putting in God. They see gold, not God, as the way to secure their future. This is as true today as it was back in Timothy's day. Look at the rest of 1 Timothy 6:9-10: "People who want to get rich fall into temptation and a trap and into many foolish and harmful desires that plunge men into ruin and destruction. For the love of money is a root of all kinds of evil. Some people, eager for money, have wandered from the faith and pierced themselves with many griefs." This statement from Timothy perfectly captures the tragedy of compulsive gambling as a way to attain wealth.

Gamblers often equate wealth with security, but money is false secu-rity. Jesus told us, "Do not store up for yourselves treasures on earth, where moth and rust destroy, and where thieves break in and steal. But store up for yourselves treasures in heaven, where moth and rust do not destroy, and where thieves do not break in and steal. For where your treasure is, there your heart will be also" (Matthew 6:19-21). The heart of the gambler is consumed with storing up earthly treasure, not heav-enly treasure. Unable to serve both God and money, the gambler chooses to serve money.

God asks us to look to him as the source of our physical needs, our daily bread, because he wants us to remember him as the source of our life. Wealth can blind us to our need for him. If we are satisfied with an ability to provide for our own earthly needs, we may forget our inability to provide for our spiritual needs. It is not by accident that Jesus says, "I tell you the truth, it is hard for a rich man to enter the kingdom of heaven. Again I tell you, it is easier for a camel to go through the eye of a needle than for a rich man to enter the kingdom of God" (Matthew 19:23-24). Content with wealth to supply our earthly needs, we grow apathetic to God's kingdom, blind to our spiritual poverty.

Where is the hope in this? After saying how hard it is to be wealthy and spiritually rich, too, "Jesus looked at them and said, 'With man this is impossible, but with God all things are possible'" (Matthew 19:26). God is aware of our physical needs and the needs of our families. He reminds us in Matthew 6 not to worry about what we will eat or drink or what we will wear. He reminds us that God knows we need those things and we are important enough to God for him to provide those things for us. Instead, we are told to "seek first his kingdom and his righteousness, and all these things will be given to you as well" (Matthew 6:33). The sin is not in having money. The sin is in giving to money what rightly belongs to God.

So what does a need for money teach us about God? It teaches us to look to God alone to fill our needs, both physical and spiritual. Why should we choose something so elusive, so odds-defying as a game of chance, to have our physical needs met? God gives us surety and a promise that if we will seek his kingdom—the spiritual—first, he will provide for the physical. Trusting in God to provide is really no gamble at all.

Practical Steps

Gambling encourages reliance on money. Relying on God instead of money can be difficult. Even devoted Christians might balk at the Old Testament tradition of giving a tenth of one's gross income to the Lord. Money, which translates into power in this culture, is difficult to give up.

Look at the story of David and the threshing floor at the end of the book of 2 Samuel. David was looking for a place to build an altar to the Lord, and he offered to buy Araunah's threshing floor. Araunah offered to give David the threshing floor without cost, but David said no. He paid Araunah and said, "I will not sacrifice to the LORD my God burnt offerings that cost me nothing" (2 Samuel 24:24). He said, in essence, "I will not give to the Lord that which costs me nothing." For some of us, that is all we are willing to give to God. But when we truly give our lives to God, he asks us to make sacrifices. Giving up control of our money is difficult. It costs us something. Yet we also gain a great deal as we rely on God to provide security in our lives.

Not spending money on gambling is a huge step, but it is not the only step. God instructs us to contribute financially to the church. Contributing to the work of the saints is part of his plan for us. What portion of your income you give is between you and God, but he asks us to give a part.

When you were gambling, you probably could always find money to gamble with. As you begin to contribute to the church, you may find that money seems harder to come by. It will be tempting to try to fix your financial problems by putting all of your money into debt repayment or settling bills. God wants us to be responsible and pay our bills, but he also instructs us to contribute a portion of our income to the work of the church.

Both of these tasks can be difficult to accomplish without faith in God—and a budget. For help crafting a workable budget for your family, you can take advantage of a variety of Christian financial services, such as Christian Financial Concepts, founded by Larry Burkett. Burkett's helpful books, workbooks, and tapes are available from most bookstores. Also many churches have members who can provide counsel on how to manage your money.

Another way to get help in budgeting is to contact the Consumer Credit Counseling Service. These volunteers work with people who are trying to reestablish or rescue their financial foundations and avoid bankruptcy. Together they can work with you to craft a budget, reduce the amount of your monthly debt load, pay off your creditors, and reestablish your credit.

Remember as you craft your budget that your first item under the disbursement column should be your contribution to God. Trust him to sustain you as you obey his word. Expect him to work through your finances and your giving and be thankful when he does. Be open to the spiritual lessons he has to teach you through money. Gambling and the way you used your money used to be a curse that trapped you. When we allow God to direct the use of our money, we receive his blessing and find freedom.

GAMBLING FOR POSITION

Being "one in a million" does not always make a person feel special. Often it leaves us feeling insignificant and invisible. Lost in the crowd, some of us seek markers to show where we have been and affirm who we are. The source of this struggle is a basic human need to be affirmed.

Some use gambling as a way to meet their need for affirmation. Gambling is their preferred platform to rise above the crowd, to avoid being unnoticed amidst the throng. Each bet is a cry for affirmation in an endless quest to climb up on the shoulders of those they beat. As the crowd around them shifts and moves, their lofty position is inevitably short-lived. Soon they need to scramble upward with another bet. Up and down, up and down, their lives become an endless competition, often waged against those closest to them.

Bettering ourselves against others is a bitter activity. It pits one person against another in a perpetual cycle of one-upmanship. We begin to see family and friends as human stepladders instead of companions. The perpetual wager might gain ascendancy over the crowd, but at a terrible, lonely cost. Eventually, most people resent being stepped on and they move on.

As the music faded and the congregation sat down, Caleb could see Mike make his way to the podium. Caleb had to admit he'd never felt close to Mike. Everything about him seemed to be in place. Caleb always felt a little less sure about himself when he compared himself to Mike. It was quite a shock then to hear Mike begin to give his testimony about how God had rescued him from an addiction to pornography. Caleb was stunned. He was stunned at Mike for admitting this problem and stunned at himself for the feelings of empathy and compassion surfacing inside him. There had been a day not so long ago when Caleb would have taken Mike's honesty and gladly shoved it back in his face. Not anymore. Being so intimately aware of his own redemption, Caleb praised God for Mike's.

A better way to fill our need for affirmation is to serve others and not compete against them, to act in humility and not seek earthly gain. Paradoxically, our self-worth is found in affirming others rather than ourselves. Affirmation is found in the topsy-turvy example of Christ, "who, being in very nature God, did not consider equality with God something to be grasped, but made himself nothing, taking the very nature of a servant, being made in human likeness. And being found in appearance as a man, he humbled himself and became obedient to death—even death on a cross! Therefore God exalted him to the highest place and gave him the name that is above every name, that at the name of Jesus every knee should bow, in heaven and on earth and under the earth, and every tongue confess that Jesus Christ is Lord, to the glory of God the Father" (Philippians 2:6-11).

We may believe wagering will fill our need for affirmation because it exalts us above others. Nothing could be further from the truth. Christ tells us, "Whoever exalts himself will be humbled, and whoever humbles himself will be exalted" (Matthew 23:12). Who exalts us? Scripture says that God is the one who sets the lowly on high (Job 5:11) and rebukes the kings of the earth (Psalm 2). When Christ voluntarily humbled himself, God exalted him.

If God wants us to humble ourselves, why were we created with a need for affirmation? And why is that need so strong that people treat each other badly just so they can feel good about themselves? Before affirmation comes humility. Christ willingly humbled himself and calls us to be like him. Our desire to be lifted up contributes to our motivation to be like Christ and endure humility. The author of Hebrews tell us, "Let us fix our eyes on Jesus, the author and perfecter of our faith, who for the joy set before him endured the cross, scorning its shame, and sat down at the right hand of the throne of God. Consider him who endured such opposition from sinful men, so that you will not grow weary and lose heart" (Hebrews 12:2-3). God created us with a desire for affirmation so we would seek out the affirmation of God.

Perpetual gamblers have grown weary and lost heart. Opposition has persuaded them to give up seeking affirmation from God and instead seek the transitory affirmation of others. All of us sometimes settle for people's affirmation instead of God's. We become like the Pharisees who "loved praise from men more than praise from God" (John 12:43). It does not seem like a safe bet to endure the shame of men on the chimera of future glory. Paradoxically, it's the surest bet of all, because God himself guarantees the outcome when we are lifted up just as Christ was.

Practical Steps

In our pain we often think that God has a finite number of rewards. If someone wins, then someone else must lose. At all costs, we must not be considered a loser. Therefore, when someone else wins, we feel threatened. When someone else loses, we feel relieved because we have hope that maybe we'll win.

This thinking is wrong for a number of reasons, but two stand out: (1) God doesn't work that way, and (2) it pits us against each other. God does not grade on a curve. Another person's sin does not bring us any closer to heaven. God has made us allies, not adversaries, in the world. We are to be like Christ and lift each other up, not look for ways to tear each other down.

One of the best ways to gain empathy for other people is to pray for them. By petitioning God on their behalf, we become their champion, their advocate. We put ourselves in their place and gain an understanding of their life and struggle.

Another excellent way to gain empathy for other people is to learn more about grace. So often we assume that God's grace is provided in buckets for the sins of others and in thimbles for our own. Realizing the truth about grace and how God measures sin can be a startling revelation. Understanding grace opens us up to the character of God and reveals the source of true empathy for other people.[1]

THE BATTLE FOR CONTROL

Every spiritual battle that wages in every human being begins with the will. Simply put, we want to be in control of our lives. Rebelliously, we resent having to submit to a control that is not our own. This deep loathing of an authority outside of ourselves taints all of our relationships. Submission has become almost an obscenity in our culture.

Wealth is often considered one way to exercise control over our lives. The more money we have, the more control we appear to have over our lives and the lives of others. Wealth means power, and power means control.

Many people will work tirelessly to garner wealth for themselves, believing this wealth will allow them to control their circumstances. Jesus told a parable that illustrates the folly of this thinking:

The ground of a certain rich man produced a good crop. He thought to himself, "What shall I do? I have no place to store my crops."

Then he said, "This is what I'll do. I will tear down my barns and build bigger ones, and there I will store all my grain and my goods. And I'll say to myself, 'You have plenty of good things laid up for many years. Take life easy; eat, drink and be merry.'"

But God said to him, "You fool! This very night your life will be demanded from you. Then who will get what you have prepared for yourself?"

This is how it will be with anyone who stores up things for himself but is not rich toward God. (Luke 12:16-21)

Those who gamble for control want not only the easy life reflected in this parable, they want it without the necessity of having to plant crops or build barns! They define the easy life within a warped context of this parable: eat, drink, and be merry. Nowhere does the thought of work enter into this happy picture. The control they seek through gambling and wealth is the control to obtain the easy life without the necessity of work. They detest submission so much, even submitting within a job environment is loathsome.

Caleb watched tears track down Molly's cheeks as Mike poured out the story of God's victory over his shame. In the middle of Mike's testimony, Caleb felt a wave of cold fear. Within Mike's life, he saw a vision of his old self. Through his use of pornography, Mike admitted he was seeking total control over his sexual desires and gratification. With a stab of insight, Caleb realized that is what he had been doing with his own addiction to gambling. He'd been trying to establish control over his own life through money. How could he condemn Mike? They both pursued the same thing. The need

for control drove them to engage in behaviors they thought would bring
them satisfaction but only left them bereft of the control they sought. The
fear Caleb felt was from realizing how close he'd come to losing control
completely.

What could a desire for control at this level possibly say about God?
Why would God allow us to want so much control? Try looking at it this
way: Who controls the universe? Whose hand was it that controlled the
formation of this world? By whose authority did night and day form?
Whose word controlled the seas? God is in control. God is sovereign.
When we sin we put ourselves in the place of God. We yearn for self-
control because we listen to the lie, like Adam and Eve did, that we can
be God, we can have control. God allows us to sin because he wants us
to turn to him freely. He gives us control so we can choose to turn that
control over to him.

Choosing to trust ourselves to exercise control over our lives, instead
of giving up control to God, produces obsessive and destructive behaviors. Inherently, we realize that we are incompetent to exercise control,
yet in our stubbornness we refuse to yield control to God. We are left
with only our incompetent selves, tense and anxious. To lessen this tension and anxiety, gamblers seek out wealth—a substitute for God's sovereignty in their lives.

Practical Steps

This world is an uncertain place where controlling your situation can
appear to be a wise move. Gambling dangles the carrot of wealth, of control, in front of the gambler, yet it never delivers. Once you have
accepted this truth, take stock of your life. Examine the ways you exert
your own control. Think about which of those areas you would give up
to God's control and which areas you are unwilling to concede to him.
How does the thought of giving up control make you feel?

Begin a plan to relinquish that control to God bit by bit. Start with something that does not panic you. Maybe it's something you'd truly be glad to give over to God. Make a point each day to specifically give up that area of control to God. Pray about it. Meditate about it. Search for scriptures in your quiet times with God to give you strength to follow through with your commitment to give this area to him.

As you work through the areas of your life, one of the most helpful things you can do is to keep a journal. Chronicle your struggles and your victories. Read it over daily, if necessary, to remind yourself of God's faithfulness in the small things, whenever you are faced with giving up control over a big thing.

Sometimes being accountable to someone else provides the motivation we need to give up control to God. Consider finding a prayer partner, an accountability group, or an e-mail partner. Choose wisely a committed, strong Christian who can help you in your desire to cede control to God. Choose those who will confront you when necessary and support you when needed.

Giving over control to God is a lifelong process. Each of us has sin strongholds in our lives where we hoard our need for control. Through maturity in the faith and experiencing God in our lives, God is able to pry us, finger by finger, away from our death grip on those intractable sins. The only way to lose out altogether is to give up. Each day God's mercies are new, and we can always try again.

GAMBLING FOR COMFORT

With all of this anxiety and tension in our lives produced by our disobedience and rebellion against God, is it any wonder we also have such a need for comfort? God created us for personal connection. In a bizarre twist of this need, many people gamble compulsively to feel they are part of a "community." Within this gambling fellowship they know and are known by others. Outside of the realm of gambling, a group such as this has another name: the church.

The moment the service concluded, Caleb found himself working his way toward Mike, who was standing at the front. When he reached him, he didn't say a word but just grasped him tightly around the shoulders. Mike's arms eagerly returned the embrace, and for a moment nothing was said. "Thank you, Mike," Caleb was finally able to say. Right then, several others made their way up to Mike and began to pat him on the back or say something encouraging to him. Watching Mike and the reaction from the congregation, Caleb realized he was looking at himself. In wonder, he said to himself, "I'm really not alone anymore."

God created within us all a need to be part of a community. We are physical, spiritual, and relational beings. Relationships matter. We enjoy being part of groups. One is lonely, but many are comforting. For some, quantity is more important than quality. In other words, any group will do.

God doesn't want us to settle for less. He has in mind for us a remarkable group joined in common purpose. Within this group he provides substitutes for our damaged relationships. Within this group, he provides gifts and talents to give the group meaning and purpose outside of itself. Within this group, he mandates love, acceptance, forgiveness, admonishment, encouragement, and tenderness. He loves this group so much, when he looks at it, he sees the body of his Son. He loves this group so much, his very Spirit inhabits it. He loves this group—the church—so much, he calls it the bride of Christ.

Are you lonely? Go to God. "God sets the lonely in families" (Psalm 68:6). Are you grieving? Go to God. "Blessed are those who mourn, for they will be comforted" (Matthew 5:4). Are you anxious for companions? Go to God. "A man of many companions may come to ruin, but there is a friend who sticks closer than a brother" (Proverbs 18:24). God knows you need friendship. He knows that giving up gambling sounds difficult because it may mean giving up friends. But chances are you won't find a close friend next to you at a slot machine or behind the bar at the cardroom or on the bus en route to the casino. A close friend won't ask you to compromise your other relationships, your money, your health for gambling. A close friend won't always compete with you. A close friend will want healing for you and will draw you closer to God, the source of true comfort.

God provided the church as a way to meet our need for companionship. When people who are lonely or grieving or bored turn to the fellowship of gamblers to exclusively meet their comfort needs, they show a disrespect for God's provision for their needs through the church. First Peter 2:17 reminds us to "show proper respect to everyone: Love the brotherhood of believers." Love the church by placing your trust in the church to fill your comfort needs.

Our need for relationship reflects God's character. We are created to want relationship because he wants a relationship with us. He demonstrated his own desire for companionship with us through the sacrifice of his Son, Jesus. Before Christ died, we were estranged and separated from God; our relationship with him was broken. Christ's sacrifice was necessary to bring us back into relationship with God. He wants us to be in relationship with him. The need he gave us for relationship fits his own.

Practical Steps

We all want to be loved. Gambling offers an artificial community where love is found—not love of people but love of money.

It is good to experience God alone through the company of our own thoughts or through the majesty of God's creation. It is also important, however, to experience God with other people. God speaks to us as we commune with his Spirit but he also speaks to us through the words, thoughts, emotions, and actions of others. Being part of a church allows us to experience him more fully. There is nothing like the awesome wonder of God's physical creation to draw us closer to him, and the people around us are also part of his creation. We may want to commune with nature to find God, but we don't need to overlook his living, breathing, majesty standing next to us.

If you do not have a church home, find a congregation where you can belong. Be open to becoming a part of God's family and putting up with myriad brothers, sisters, uncles, cousins, aunts, grandparents, and children in the faith. You won't always get your own way, but that's okay. Sometimes what you want to happen is not what should happen. Together you and the people you talk and pray and worship with will learn more about the character of God.

GOD-GIVEN NEEDS

Our needs are strong. Unmet needs are stronger still. Gambling promises to meet our needs, but it continually deprives us of lasting fulfillment. The promise of having a strong need met only accentuates the void when that need is not filled at all. When this happens we can choose to become angry at God for making us with needs in the first place. We can attempt to deny that we have needs, only to confront them at every turn. To find healing, we need to acknowledge our needs and turn to God alone to fill them. Our needs are designed to draw us closer to God. Our needs are designed to break through our walls of self-reliance and motivate us to seek the Lord.

Section 3 Follow-Up

As individuals, we craft reasons and motivations to gamble. As a culture, we choose to focus on the rewards of gambling and overlook the costs. In each of these two situations, we are in charge. We decide. We choose. Healing will come when we give control over gambling to God. We cede control but gain hope.

Consider the following questions. As before, write down your answers on a separate piece of paper. Be as specific and honest as possible.

1. Before you read this book, did you view your gambling or the gambling of someone else as an almost hopeless situation? How do you feel now?

2. If you feel less hope than before, identify the areas you feel are most hopeless. Why do you consider them hopeless? Write down the specific reasons for this feeling of hopelessness.

3. As you look over these reasons to lose hope, pray over each one. Ask God to provide you with insight into how he is going to overcome each situation and every reason for hopelessness. Open your heart to his answer.

4. If you are feeling more hopeful about your own gambling or the gambling of a loved one, write down the first action you are going to take to make this hope a reality.

5. Pray for the courage to take that first step. Ask God to show you further steps you can take to regain control over your life or to help someone else who has a problem with gambling.

6. As you consider your own gambling or the gambling of someone you love, is there one thing you'd like to cry out about to God? Is there one truth you feel compelled to confess to him and to yourself? Whatever it is, confess it.

7. Regardless of whether you are a compulsive gambler, what is God telling you about the gambling you engage in? Is there room for change in your attitudes about gambling?

8. Are you afraid to hope that your gambling or the gambling of someone you love can change? Are you fearful of getting your hopes up, only to be disappointed in yourself or a loved one again? Confess your fear to God. Ask him to give you courage and a resilient spirit.

9. Are you ready to change? If the answer is yes, pour your heart out to God and ask him to renew it.

10. If the answer is no, don't try to lie to God. Be honest about your feelings; God knows them anyway. Ask God to change your heart. Ask him to do whatever it takes to reveal to you the destructive nature of your gambling. Be prepared for him to answer.

11. If your answer is both no and yes, do not quit trying because of the struggle. Continue to give control to God, step by step— inch by inch if necessary. Spend at least as much time thinking about God as you think about gambling. Truly desire for God to win this battle for your heart's affection and he will.

AFTERWORD

Let me add one final personal note about gambling. I have learned a lot myself in writing and researching this book. After this preparation:

I am convinced more than ever of the detrimental effects of gambling on this culture and on individuals.

I am concerned about the future of our young people in the face of the strong temptations gambling presents.

I am outraged over the ways the gambling industry exploits the elderly and the poor.

As I look at the overwhelming array of forces gambling represents in society today, I give this battle over to God.

I am praying for those who pick up this book. After reading the book:

May God reveal to us the truth of gambling.

May he strengthen our resolve to choose what is right.

May he forgive us when we choose what is wrong.

May he always remind us in his power to reconcile, to renew, to change.

May he fill our hearts with hope.

May these statements serve as a final word of encouragement to you. Our God is a God of hope!

Appendix A

Gambling Myths and Biblical Realities

Insights from Solomon

One of the realities of gambling is the elusive nature of its reward. One minute you're rich; another minute you're destitute. Wealth and poverty exist within the chance draw of a card, the lucky roll of a die, the timely pull of a handle, the fortunate purchase of a ticket. Gambling is a shaky foundation for wealth and happiness. Yet our culture touts gambling as an acceptable road to wealth and happiness. Society makes a shaky foundation appear sturdy.

This illusion, promoted and promulgated by outward cultural influences and inward human desires, lies at the heart of gambling's dichotomy. In truth, what gambling promises and what it delivers are worlds apart. Wisdom comes in separating the reality from the myth. This is not always easy.

Gambling would not have such a hold over the culture, including Christians, if it did not resonate with the wisdom of this world: Wealth is power, borrowing is easy, envy is empowering, greed will meet our needs, fantasies are visionary, instant gratification is a right, control is possible, pride is noble. The force of these myths is powerful and persistent.

Christians succumb to culture's siren song just as non-Christians do. We get turned around in our thinking and begin to look at things from an opposite point of view of the truth. In this turned-around condition, it is difficult to see what the real truth is. It is difficult to *want* to see what the real truth is. We become convinced that if our belief is strong, it is also correct.

This is not a new phenomenon. "There is a way that seems right to a man, but in the end it leads to death," says the wise writer Solomon in Proverbs 14:12. Perhaps more than any other writer in Scripture, Solomon tackles head-on this turned-around way of looking at what is meaningful and what is meaningless. The cultural messages in his day were similar to today's messages. He faced questions of money and power, greed and gratification, envy and pride. Within the writings of two Old Testament books, Ecclesiastes and Proverbs, Solomon recorded God's truth and wisdom. He set the record straight about what God considers valuable and what God knows has no value. He set the record straight about what is myth and what is reality. Contrast for yourself the myths of gambling to what God reveals. The differences are startling.

Myth: Wealth Is Power

One of the most powerful hooks of gambling is the promise of wealth. At the heart of most gambling is the acquisition of money. Easy money. Instant money. Effortless money. Simply, money. The messages of gambling play to the turned-around view that wealth is the solution to life's problems.

Solomon, arguably one of the wealthiest men in history, records a different truth: Wealth is meaningless. You might say, "Yeah, he could say that because he was wealthy!" and you couldn't be more correct. He could come to this conclusion because he *was* wealthy. "I amassed silver and gold for myself, and the treasure of kings and provinces," Solomon writes. "Yet when I surveyed all that my hands had done and what I had toiled to achieve, everything was meaningless, a chasing after the wind" (Ecclesiastes 2:8,11). Having wealth, Solomon understood how little money actually delivered in relation to its grand promises. He could separate the reality of money from the myth of wealth.

In the book of Proverbs, Solomon gives several simple statements about the value of wealth. He comes to the conclusion that it is a futile way to secure happiness. Contrary to what the world says, wealth is elusive and transitory. The benefits of wealth are an illusion, a smoke screen of stability and security.

Reality: Riches Are Untrustworthy

"Whoever trusts in his riches will fall, but the righteous will thrive like a green leaf" (Proverbs 11:28). Gambling asks people to trust in the myth that wealth is the only way out of their problems, money the only way to fulfill their needs. This scripture reveals the reality of riches: If you trust in them, you will fall. Not might, not may, not could—*will* fall. Sufficiency, by contrast, is gained only through Christ. When we trust in Christ to supply our needs, we thrive like a verdant leaf.

Reality: Riches Cost Something

"A man's riches may ransom his life, but a poor man hears no threat" (Proverbs 13:8). One of the truths Solomon learned about wealth is that it costs something. When people look to riches to save them, to ransom their lives, they live in fear of losing that wealth. Compulsive gamblers are all too familiar with this reality. They live under the constant threat—and reality—of lost riches. With each wager the potential of both winning and losing hangs over them.

Reality: A Fool and His Money Are Soon Parted

"Of what use is money in the hand of a fool, since he has no desire to get wisdom?" (Proverbs 17:16). Gambling and the quick riches it promises are pitted against the slow task of gaining wisdom. Wisdom, however, has eternal value. Money could be gone the next day or never come at all. Money flies in and out of the gambler's hands. Once in hand, it has no value because it comes with no wisdom. Countless times, gamblers admit that anything they win is only seed money for their next wager. Present winnings are only future bets. The car may be falling apart, the rent overdue, the children without lunch money, and the creditors calling on the phone, but money won through gambling is devoted only to further gambling. In this context, the compulsive gambler is a fool because he is choosing wealth over wisdom.

Reality: Wealth Alone Is Worthless

"Humility and the fear of the LORD bring wealth and honor and life" (Proverbs 22:4). Wealth is only meaningful when it is accompanied by honor and life. These three things are obtained through humility and fear of the Lord. We can't construe this, however, as a spiritual formula for secular prosperity. God does not always define wealth the way we do. After all, God considers weeds more valuable than fine clothing. "And why do you worry about clothes? See how the lilies of the field grow. They do not labor or spin. Yet I tell you that not even Solomon in all his splendor was dressed like one of these" (Matthew 6:28-29). By allowing God to define the terms, through humility and reverent fear, we will obtain wealth and honor and life.

Reality: You Can Wear Yourself Out Getting Rich

"Do not wear yourself out to get rich; have the wisdom to show restraint" (Proverbs 23:4). If there is one thing compulsive gamblers lack, it is restraint. Through their gambling behaviors they are literally wearing themselves out to get rich. For them, becoming rich is worth the exhaustion. God instead asks us to have the wisdom to show restraint. By wearing ourselves out to become rich, we never have the energy we need to do the important things in life. Family, jobs, and relationships are all sacrificed in the pursuit of the big win. This task is exhausting and gives nothing of true value back.

Reality: Wealth Doesn't Last

"Cast but a glance at riches, and they are gone, for they will surely sprout wings and fly off to the sky like an eagle" (Proverbs 23:5). This passage perfectly encapsulates the "luck of the draw." Gambling's wealth is here today and gone tomorrow. It truly does take wing and fly away on the winds of the next wager. Gamblers erroneously feel that wealth, as transitory and fickle as it is, holds the key to security.

MYTH: BORROWING IS EASY

So compelling is the desire for wealth that many people will actually do the opposite—go into debt—to acquire it. Casinos and cardrooms provide credit machines and borrowing mechanisms to allow gamblers to not only spend what they have but spend what they don't have. Borrowing, or credit, is seen as a legitimate strategy to keep gambling. Going into debt to become wealthy is another example of turned-around thinking. The world says borrowing to gamble is acceptable. Solomon learned otherwise.

Reality: Debt Is Oppressive

"The rich rule over the poor, and the borrower is servant to the lender" (Proverbs 22:7). The problems of many compulsive gamblers do not end when they leave the casino or the cardroom. If they gambled on credit, not only did they lose all their present money, they lost part of their future earnings. The more dire their financial condition, the greater the impulse to turn to gambling as a way out. The more they gamble, the more they lose and the more they enter into servitude.

Scripture is very clear about the dangers of going into debt. God knows the oppression that results when one person owes another. Para-doxically, one person goes into debt in order to obtain wealth and power and ends up a debtor, without wealth or power, at the mercy of the lender. Again, what gambling promises and what it delivers are worlds apart.

Reality: Debt Must Be Repaid

"Do not be a man who strikes hands in pledge or puts up security for debts; if you lack the means to pay, your very bed will be snatched from under you" (Proverbs 22:26-27). God cares about the oppressed. He is concerned about lenders taking unfair advantage of borrowers. He also knows the realities of the world. Gamblers who max out their credit cards cannot cry out against the credit companies. After all, no one forced them to accept the credit offered. It was their decision. Nor can Christians who gamble on credit protest of their ignorance—God, thou-sands of years ago, gave these words as a warning. God understands the way people are. God knows that he is merciful and we are not. If you owe someone in this world, you are expected to pay.

MYTH: ENVY IS EMPOWERING

Envy is at the root of many gamblers' desire for wealth. They see the prosperity of others and are envious. They see what others have and want it. Not only do they want what others have, they want it now. Envy may fuel their desire for wealth, but it takes out of a person more than it gives. Envy isn't empowering, it's draining.

Reality: Envy Is Meaningless

"And I saw that all labor and all achievement spring from man's envy of his neighbor. This too is meaningless, a chasing after the wind" (Ecclesi-astes 4:4). God wants us to love our neighbor, not love our neighbor's things. Envy is a profitless motivation to acquire wealth. As soon as you obtain what one person has, you are sure to notice what another person has. Envy is never satisfied; there will always be someone who has more than you.

Reality: You Are Like the One You Envy

"I have seen something else under the sun: The race is not to the swift or the battle to the strong, nor does food come to the wise or wealth to the brilliant or favor to the learned; but time and chance happen to them all" (Ecclesiastes 9:11). From the outside looking in, it may seem that other people are somehow special. That through special circumstances, they have been able to obtain what you have not. It can appear as if others are somehow blessed and you are somehow not. Lottery winnings, in particular, are advertised as a way to balance this inequity. Some Christians believe that winnings should be used by God to redress the unfairness they perceive in their own situation. They grow resentful when God does not intervene. In reality, God is at work in your life as much as he is at work in others' lives. As Solomon writes, good and bad things happen to each of us. Other people are likely looking at you and wishing they could have what you have. Often it is difficult to see the blessings God has given us when looking through the eyes of envy.

Reality: Envy Sucks You Dry

"A heart at peace gives life to the body, but envy rots the bones" (Proverbs 14:30). Envy is a heartless taskmaster. Never satisfied, it spurs a person to bitterness. With envy comes a feeling that others are blessed and you are cursed. It is not merely that others seem to prosper but that you seem to never get ahead. This bitterness, scripture says, "rots the bones." God never intended us to live this way. Instead, we are to strive for a heart at peace. A contented heart has no room for envy. A contented heart has no room for the false promises of gambling.

MYTH: GREED WILL SATISFY MY NEEDS

Just as envy is never satisfied, neither is greed. Greed, by definition, is not about need but about want. Greed whispers that if some is good, more is better and even more is better still. Satisfaction never comes, waiting for the accumulation of more. The promise is never delivered on. The drive to acquire more and more continues relentlessly.

Gambling is perfectly tailored to greed. The payoffs promised get higher and higher. It isn't enough to try for a million dollars anymore, now it's ten million. Winning a small amount isn't enough to satisfy. The small winnings are wagered against a larger payoff. The level where you will be satisfied constantly moves upward, contentment an ever-moving target. Win ten and you want to win twenty. Win twenty and you want to win a hundred. Win a hundred and you want to win a thousand. And on it goes.

Reality: Greed Is Never Satisfied

"Whoever loves money never has money enough; whoever loves wealth is never satisfied with his income. This too is meaningless" (Ecclesiastes 5:10). The perverse side of human greed is that no matter how much you have, it's never enough. Compulsive gamblers tell stories of gaining incredible amounts of money—for a short time. Though the amounts were significant, greed screamed to try to gain even more. The more they won, the more they wanted. The more they wanted, the more they gambled. The more they gambled, the more they lost. In other words, the more they won, the more they lost. This is the terrible paradox of compulsive gambling.

Reality: Greed Can Lead to Theft

"Ill-gotten treasures are of no value, but righteousness delivers from death" (Proverbs 10:2). When greed takes over a person's heart, wealth is an end in itself. Some gamblers will cheat and manipulate others out of their money. In an elaborate excuse for this behavior, they rationalize that if the person was foolish enough to lose money then it's their fault. In fact, some people take perverse pleasure not only in the wealth obtained from others, but in the way that wealth is obtained. God says what is obtained in this way is of no true value. Money may be gained, but relationships are lost.

Reality: Greed Feeds Self

"One man gives freely, yet gains even more; another withholds unduly, but comes to poverty" (Proverbs 11:24). When greed takes hold of our hearts, there is little room for compassion or empathy. We become obsessed with obtaining things for self, not in giving to others. Few people gamble in order to give their winnings away.

Now some will attempt to barter with God. They may say, "God, if you will allow me to win this lottery, I will give a full 10 percent to good works." In their hearts, the tithe is really a payment. It is the cost of obtaining the rest of the money. If they were honest, they would see their tithe for what it is—a tax on the winnings, not a selfless gift to God. Gamblers counting on divine intervention for their behaviors should be aware of an important truth: God cannot be bribed. When we are greedy for money, we are greedy for our own sake.

Reality: Greed Brings Trouble

"A greedy man brings trouble to his family, but he who hates bribes will live" (Proverbs 15:27). One of the most heartrending aspects for those who participated in the National Gambling Impact Study Commission was listening to the stories of how gambling devastated relationships. The gambler's greed truly brings trouble to the family. Spouses and children suffer when a gambler is out of control. Families and friends suffer also when they realize that the gambler loves gambling more than them. This truth can devastate their lives.

Reality: Greed Settles for Crumbs

"He who is full loathes honey, but to the hungry even what is bitter tastes sweet" (Proverbs 27:7). Greed never satisfies. It never fills. It leaves a person constantly hungering for more. In a state of perpetual desire, the greedy accept even what is bitter—compulsive gambling—and think it tastes sweet. Ravenous for more, they consume the bitter fruit of gambling and proclaim to themselves and those around them about "how sweet it is." Turned around in her thinking, the gambler is willing to settle for less.

Reality: Greed Exacts a Price

"A faithful man will be richly blessed, but one eager to get rich will not go unpunished" (Proverbs 28:20). Not only do the greedy accept what is bitter and call it sweet, they reject what is sweet and call it tasteless. The gambler, eager to get rich, does not give time and energy to increasing her faith. Wealth is a god, and gambling is a form of worship. If the goal is worldly gain, then spiritual pursuits are valueless. Greed skews an understanding of the ways things work. In God's will, the one who pursues faith is enriched and the one who pursues riches is punished. Christ counseled us to "seek first his kingdom and his righteousness" (Matthew 6:33).

The Reality: Greed Produces Unrest

"A greedy man stirs up dissension, but he who trusts in the LORD will prosper" (Proverbs 28:25). Never satisfied, greedy people cannot stand the contentment of others. Contentment only points out the discontent in their own hearts. Stirring the pot, the greedy often look for a way to prosper from the turmoil of others. Those gamblers who constantly wager against those around them are greedy people stirring up dissension. Through manipulation and humiliation, they disturb the contentment of others.

MYTH: FANTASY IS VISIONARY

When we turn to gambling to solve our problems, we end up doing little more than chasing our dreams. In the turned-around way of this world, gamblers see the fantasy of wealth and prestige more than the realities of gambling. These dreams are so powerful, they actually take on substance in the mind of the gambler. With each bet, the gambler believes this time she will win. She can see and taste and smell the win just around the corner. The only way to avoid the win she believes is inevitable is to stop gambling. So she continues, gaining assurance from every failure that success is just a wager away.

In the words of an old saying, "If wishes were horses, beggars would ride." Gamblers spend a great deal of time mounted on the backs of their own desires. They would rather spend time fantasizing about obtaining money than actually working to make money. Not much has changed in this regard from the time of Solomon.

Reality: Fantasies Are Empty

"He who works his land will have abundant food, but he who chases fantasies lacks judgment" (Proverbs 12:11). It is so much easier to talk about what you will do than actually to do it. Doing requires work. All talking requires is hot air.

Reality: Fantasies Are Unfulfilled

"The sluggard craves and gets nothing, but the desires of the diligent are fully satisfied" (Proverbs 13:4). Fantasies about gambling do nothing to fill the craving for winning. God reminds us that fantasies gain nothing, but diligence delivers.

Reality: Fantasies Aren't Real

"A simple man believes anything, but a prudent man gives thought to his steps" (Proverbs 14:15). When the desire to believe something is strong enough, the belief takes on a life of its own. Unfortunately, the belief that a win is just a wager away reveals a gambler who literally will believe anything. The facts of gambling attest to the opposite.

Reality: Fantasies Produce Poverty

"All hard work brings a profit, but mere talk leads only to poverty" (Proverbs 14:23). Many people who gamble simply wish to avoid the necessity of working hard. This scripture reveals that it is work, not wishes, that brings reward.

Reality: Fantasies Leave You Unprepared

"A sluggard does not plow in season; so at harvest time he looks but finds nothing" (Proverbs 20:4). If you believe in the fantasy that the next wager is going to bring you wealth, why worry about preparing for tomorrow? As far as you are concerned, the win will fix everything. When the win doesn't come and things aren't fixed, the dreamer is left totally unprepared.

Reality: Fantasies Don't Put Food on the Table

"He who works his land will have abundant food, but the one who chases fantasies will have his fill of poverty" (Proverbs 28:19). This scripture rightly says that fantasies are things to be chased. They are chased but never caught. And while the gambler is off chasing her fantasies, her plate is left empty.

Each of these wise sayings points out a similar reality: Work produces; fantasizing does not. Mere work often appears dull and boring, unfulfilling, to the gambler. When compared with the glamour of desires and the heady rush of the big win, the reality of work is colorless and unappealing. "Why go to a boring job day after day and receive less for all that trouble than a single win at the game? Why, any day now, luck will change, and I'll have more money than I know what to do with. Any day now."

And while gamblers wait for that day, there is no motivation to work. If they do have a job, it is sneered at as a necessary evil until they hit the jackpot. If they don't have a job, why get one? Unemployed, they have more time to gamble. Unemployed, they have more time to dream.

It is good to look to the future, to hope and plan and dream. When dreams get in the way of reality, however, we must stop and consider the truth of the present.

MYTH: INSTANT GRATIFICATION IS A RIGHT

Perhaps at no other time in history has our culture had as great an expectation of instant gratification. We are permanently lodged on fast forward. The pace of our technology creates the impression that anything worth having is worth having now. The question of our time is, "Why wait?" Fast food. Instant credit. No money down. No waiting. We are becoming toddlers—wanting what we want when we want it. And if we don't get it, we scream. In our world-view, there is no value in waiting. God, timeless and the maker of time, thinks differently.

Gamblers live on a fast track. The deeper they sink into gambling behaviors, the more they slip into debt. Once debt is accumulated, pressure mounts to pay it off. The gambler wants instant credit, and the creditor wants instant restitution. The merry-go-round of winning-losing-debt-credit spins the gambler crazily out of control. Within this whirlwind of activity, the gambler is twisted and turned, buffeted and bruised. Many find themselves longing for just a few moments of peace and tranquillity amidst the chaos.

Reality: Later Is Better Than Now

"The end of a matter is better than the beginning, and patience is better than pride" (Ecclesiastes 7:8). God's answer to the chaos is peace through patience and perseverance. Patience cannot be obtained quickly or easily; it comes at the end of things. And the end of things only comes after a beginning and a middle. Patience is a progression. Pride demands things now. Patience is willing to wait for the outcome.

Many use gambling as a way to circumvent the process of attaining wealth. They want the end product of financial security without the journey required to obtain it. Gambling entices people to spend money they do not have to become rich overnight. Sadly, stories fill newscasts about lottery winners who lose their winnings almost as quickly as they won them. Without wisdom and patience gained over time, they spend their winnings without return.

Reality: Now Leads to Mistakes

"This only have I found: God made mankind upright, but men have gone in search of many schemes" (Ecclesiastes 7:29). When we make decisions quickly, we often make them incorrectly. It takes time to calculate the correct course or come to the proper conclusion about a matter. Sometimes we are unwilling to wait. Stubbornly, we strike out on our own, searching for our own fulfillment instead of waiting on God. Impatiently, we expect God to act according to our timing. When he doesn't, some people abandon him and take matters into their own hands.

This is especially true of Christians who compulsively gamble. Their faith in Jesus' redemption has made them upright. But unwilling to be patient and wait on God to provide the answer for whatever difficulty they face, they choose gambling to rescue themselves. Instead of providing relief, it only draws them closer and closer to disaster.

Reality: You Can't Always Get What You Want

"The LORD does not let the righteous go hungry but he thwarts the craving of the wicked" (Proverbs 10:3). When you are hungry, you want to eat—now. The desire is consuming and immediate. Waiting to eat can even seem painful. For those who have given their hearts over to gambling, the desire to gamble is like physical hunger. They crave gambling. Solomon reminds God's people of God's faithfulness. He will not let his children go hungry but expects us to wait on him, trusting that he is able to fill us up. When we reject waiting on God and crave the rewards of the world, God thwarts our cravings. Gamblers who gamble long enough will lose more than they win.

Someone who has given her heart over to gambling may cry out in confusion over why her situation never seems to get better. She may rail at God for not rescuing her by intervening through gambling to provide the money she needs so desperately. Her circumstances may seem so unfair, she cries out to God, "why?" The answer is found in this passage: God thwarts worldly cravings but fills up righteous hunger. If we want God to fill us up, we must seek to be filled with godly things.

Reality: Fools Rush In

"A wise man fears the LORD and shuns evil, but a fool is hotheaded and reckless" (Proverbs 14:16). Some people gamble for the sheer thrill of the moment. The rush of excitement leaves them breathless and energized. God has another term for "breathless and energized" where gambling is concerned: He would call it "hotheaded and reckless." For some, the very speed at which gambling fortunes twist and change is like rushing headlong down a mountain or racing around a racetrack or plummeting from a bungee cord toward the earth. Love of the immediate thrill captivates their heart. In search of this rush, thrill-loving Christians will compromise their values and engage in activities that take them farther from God, rather than closer. Their desire outweighs their fear of the Lord. Since the fear of the Lord is the beginning of knowledge, this kind of behavior is rightly termed foolish.

Myth: Control Is Possible

Compulsive gamblers seek control over their lives but have lost control through their gambling. Gambling promises control, but it delivers the opposite: a life out of control.

Reality: Lack of Control Leaves You Broken

"Like a city whose walls are broken down is a man who lacks self-control" (Proverbs 25:28). Gamblers seek control and find brokenness. The walls of their lives crumble around them, but they are unable to stop. Their spouses may have left them, their children may despise them, their employers may have fired them, their finances may have disappeared, but on they gamble, leaving themselves vulnerable to greed, envy, despair, and misery. Self-control is only possible as the result of living in the Spirit and ceding control to God.

MYTH: PRIDE IS NOBLE

Because our culture equates money with power and power with worth, gamblers pursue self-worth through the acquisition of money. When they win, either by making money or by making someone else lose, they feel proud. They boast about their winnings. They brag to others how they bested the person who lost. They feel they have earned the right to be proud.

Reality: Pride Is Oppressive

"All this I saw, as I applied my mind to everything done under the sun. There is a time when a man lords it over others to his own hurt" (Ecclesiastes 8:9). When one person wins a bet over another, that person obtains not only money but bragging rights—the right to boast about prowess or intellect or luck. Winning gains leverage over the other person. From that lofty position, the temptation is great to hurl insults. Even Christians elevate themselves on the backs of others. These others are ones Christ has died for as well. God calls us to lift people up, not elevate ourselves.

Reality: False Pride Is Foolish

"Do not be wise in your own eyes; fear the LORD and shun evil. This will bring health to your body and nourishment to your bones"

(Proverbs 3:7-8). We have a deep need to feel significant. Too often, this need is satisfied through pride, or being "wise in your own eyes." Pride is one of the more subtle motivations for gambling. This is especially true if you gamble on sporting events. Wagering on these kinds of events is more complicated than a random fifty-fifty outcome. Instead these wagers are calculated with facts and figures, with statistical data and encyclopedic knowledge. This type of gambling is not a game of chance as much as a game of skill. Winners, therefore, are skillful. Losers are not. Gamblers of this type seek self-pride.

Reality: Pride Doesn't Last

"Do not boast about tomorrow, for you do not know what a day may bring forth" (Proverbs 27:1). Gamblers always boast of their future winnings. When family or friends protest their behavior and bring up the past, gamblers are quick to point out the few wins among the many losses. Boastful about what tomorrow will surely bring, they set their hopes on a time that may never come.

The gambler wants to hold tomorrow in her hand. In her hand, tomorrow will bring what her heart desires: wealth, prestige, bragging rights, restitution, and even retribution. Gamblers want a genie for a god, not God Almighty. They want to be able to take him out of the box or down from the shelf and command him to craft the world according to their wishes. Yet it is God, not us, who holds tomorrow in his hand.

SHATTERING THE MYTHS

The wisdom of Solomon challenges the myths surrounding gambling. No myth is left valid. Not only is gambling for wealth shown to be meaningless, but wealth itself is shown to have no meaning. So what is meaningful? If wealth and all it provides do not give people what they need in life, what does?

The Reality of Work

Work, or toil, in God's view, can be an abundant source of joy and gladness in life. You might protest, "Yes, but you don't know my job!" True, but God does. He does not make special exceptions in these passages about which types of jobs will bring satisfaction and which won't. He even speaks of work as toilsome and, in some cases, something we don't deserve. "Now," you might be tempted to say, "he's talking about my job!"

God blesses people through their work, whatever it is. However, it is not the job itself that is the gift from the Lord but rather a person's enjoyment in and acceptance of her job. Look at these passages from Ecclesiastes. People demand that God provide them with a job they like. God, on the other hand, offers to empower people to like the job they have. These are not the same.

> A man can do nothing better than to eat and drink and find
> satisfaction in his work. This too, I see, is from the hand of God,
> for without him, who can eat or find enjoyment? To the man
> who pleases him, God gives wisdom, knowledge and happiness,
> but to the sinner he gives the task of gathering and storing up
> wealth to hand it over to the one who pleases God. This too is
> meaningless, a chasing after the wind. (Ecclesiastes 2:24-26)

> I know that there is nothing better for men than to be happy
> and do good while they live. That everyone may eat and drink,
> and find satisfaction in all his toil—this is the gift of God.
> (Ecclesiastes 3:12-13)

> So I saw that there is nothing better for a man than to enjoy
> his work, because that is his lot. For who can bring him to see
> what will happen after him? (Ecclesiastes 3:22)

> Then I realized that it is good and proper for a man to eat and
> drink, and to find satisfaction in his toilsome labor under the
> sun during the few days of life God has given him—for this is

his lot. Moreover, when God gives any man wealth and possessions, and enables him to enjoy them, to accept his lot and be
happy in his work—this is a gift of God. (Ecclesiastes 5:18-19)

There is something else meaningless that occurs on earth:
righteous men who get what the wicked deserve, and wicked
men who get what the righteous deserve. This too, I say, is
meaningless. So I commend the enjoyment of life, because
nothing is better for a man under the sun than to eat and
drink and be glad. Then joy will accompany him in his
work all the days of the life God has given him under the
sun. (Ecclesiastes 8:14-15)

Consider again that last scripture. God offers enjoyment not merely
through a specific job but through the work itself. God gives us the very
act of work as a way to find satisfaction in life. The world finds satisfaction in the *product* of work, not work itself. Yet the majority of people
gain some sense of satisfaction in what they do.

Acceptance is part of God-given satisfaction. Solomon was writing
at a time when few people had the luxury to be able to pick their jobs.
Only the very wealthy had that kind of employment freedom. People
either went into the established family trade or were slaves. Not much
choice there. Taken in historical context, these passages and this concept
are even more startling and contrary to contemporary wisdom.

While fantasy fuels much of gambling's power, discontent fuels the
flame as well. Some people view their jobs negatively and dream of being
able to walk in Monday morning, open the supervisor's door without
knocking, and give him or her an earful before saying, with intense satisfaction, "I quit!"

Granted, some do this anyway, but most are rightly fearful of being
left without a current job or a recommendation for a future one. It
might feel good for some employees to fantasize about this scenario, but
most will never do it—unless they have another source of income.

Unless, perhaps, they found a way to provide for themselves and their family without the job in question. Unless, by chance, they should win the lottery or hit the jackpot in Vegas. Then all bets are off, and the employer had better watch out!

Dissatisfaction in working is a prime motivation for people to choose to gamble. This motivation is powerful and persuasive, hooking itself deep into our desires and our resentments. Sometimes our resentments are even stronger than our desires. Gambling plays into them both.

Our God, mercifully, is more powerful and more persuasive. He is able to provide us a gift, a wellspring of happiness based around our labor. He is even able to reveal to us the joys in work itself. Many people desire to win at gambling so they can cease working altogether. God, on the other hand, sees the satisfaction to be gained from toil, even if a person already has wealth and possessions. Rather than a burdensome activity, jettisoned at the first opportunity, work has lasting value in God's eyes. As such, God warns us against the lack of a desire to work. When we are lazy, we miss out on the blessings God has given us in work.

The Reality of Diligence

"Lazy hands make a man poor, but diligent hands bring wealth" (Proverbs 10:4). Work, especially working at a difficult job, teaches people to be diligent in their labor. Diligence, practiced over time, produces the reward of wealth. In contrast to the get-rich-quick promise of gambling, diligence applied to your job and finances is an assurance of financial reward. As an added bonus, diligence learned in one area of life is transferable to others. Learn to be diligent at work and you can apply that lesson to your family life, your devotional life, your physical life. Benjamin Franklin put it this way: "Early to bed, early to rise, makes a man healthy, wealthy, and wise."

"Dishonest money dwindles away, but he who gathers money little by little makes it grow" (Proverbs 13:11). When we expend little or no effort to produce money, the money has little value. The world has a term for this kind of wealth: "Easy come, easy go." Solomon points out that ill-gotten gain, or "easy money," has a way of draining out of our hands, while patient saving grows.

This could also be called "the Proverb of Compound Interest." Each amount may appear small and insignificant, compared with the extravagant promises of gambling's payoff, but together each little amount reinforces the other, producing more than the sum of each individual part.

"The plans of the diligent lead to profit as surely as haste leads to poverty" (Proverbs 21:5). It is amazing how quickly a lifetime of savings can be gambled away and lost. In the heat of wagering, compulsive gamblers throw caution to the wind and leverage, in minutes, resources it may have taken a lifetime to accrue. Just as it takes longer to build than to destroy, it takes longer to acquire than to forfeit. Gamblers are well acquainted with this truth. A quick survey of the messages posted on the Web site for Gamblers Anonymous shows stories of vast amounts of money gained and lost, all within a few short hours.

God clearly promises that joy and gladness can be gained from work. God rewards acceptance of our jobs with satisfaction. He further shows how even small amounts, taken together, can produce great sums. Work, far from a burden, can be a source of great blessing from God.

The Reality of Judgment

Another thing is clear in the writings of Solomon: God is aware of what we do. There is no "off the clock" time with God. We belong to him at all times, whether at work or at play, whether in the night or in the day, whether engaged in positive activities or negative ones. God sees everything we do and judges the motives of our hearts.

Gambling usually brings out negative motives; compulsive gambling always does. These negative motives have been talked about before: greed, envy, bitterness, boredom, resentment, seeking after sensation.

When we gamble, those negative motives are given free rein and allowed to flow through us. When we gamble, what we feel is not hidden from God. We may be gambling in the middle of the night, hidden from view of families and friends, but God knows right where we are.

"Be happy, young man, while you are young, and let your heart give you joy in the days of your youth. Follow the ways of your heart and whatever your eyes see, but know that for all these things God will bring you to judgment" (Ecclesiastes 11:9). Today's young people are becoming ensnared in compulsive gambling behaviors. One of their excuses is that they are merely using gambling as a way to enjoy being young. From this passage it is clear that God wants young people to be happy and take joy in their youth. He also wants young people to know that youthful energy is not to be used for youthful indulgence. Even young people will be held accountable. Youth is no excuse.

"For a man's ways are in full view of the LORD, and he examines all his paths. The evil deeds of a wicked man ensnare him, the cords of his sin hold him fast" (Proverbs 5:21-22). How wonderful this passage is! How comforting to know that God is always aware of where we are with him. God examines our very steps to see if we are following him. He knows what will happen to us if we do not: Our evil deeds will ensnare us and our sin will hold us fast.

The Reality of First Fruits

Wealth is not only meaningful, it is a way to show honor to God. Money, while certainly used by some as an idol, is not evil. It is the love of money that is evil in God's sight. Instead of loving money and honoring it through our gambling, we are called to love God and honor him through our wealth.

"Honor the LORD with your wealth, with the firstfruits of all your crops; then your barns will be filled to overflowing, and your vats will brim over with new wine" (Proverbs 3:9-10). This passage is similar to the concept of losing your life in Christ in order to save it. By giving to God the first fruits, or the best, we show we trust in him to care for us. This truth runs counter to what the world says. The world teaches us to hoard what we have. God promises that if we honor him first with our wealth, he will provide for all our needs.

The Reality of True Worth

"Blessed is the man who finds wisdom, the man who gains understanding, for she is more profitable than silver and yields better returns than gold" (Proverbs 3:13-14). Gambling means trying to find silver and gold for yourself. God says that wisdom and understanding are more profitable than money. The world has already made its choice. When Christians join the world and choose money over wisdom, they call their God a liar.

"By wisdom a house is built, and through understanding it is established; through knowledge its rooms are filled with rare and beautiful treasures" (Proverbs 24:3). How many times must God reinforce this truth for us? Compulsive gambling and the relentless pursuit of material possessions tear down houses and leave them ruined. Instead, God says to seek after wisdom and allow understanding to establish your house. His word picture is exquisite: When we do, our "rooms are filled with rare and beautiful treasures." For what could be more beautiful than rooms filled with those we love?

"I love those who love me, and those who seek me find me. With me are riches and honor, enduring wealth and prosperity. My fruit is better than fine gold; what I yield surpasses choice silver" (Proverbs 8:17-19). God is an extravagant Father. It is his delight to give precious gifts to his children. Before the foundation of the world, he was prepared to give to us his only beloved Son. He created and crafted a future full of good things, and we decline. Instead, we chase after pale imitations of his gifts, rebelliously wanting to get things for ourselves. When we say no to his gifts, we say no to his blessings, his riches, and his prosperity.

The Reality of the Price

"The wages of the righteous bring them life, but the income of the wicked brings them punishment" (Proverbs 10:16). This passage admits that wickedness can supply a person with "income," but it doesn't come without a price. Some people may engage in gambling and actually come away with an income from it. But at what price? Sadly, compulsive gamblers too often pay a tremendous price for the paltry income they receive from gambling. They trade in their jobs, their families, their possessions, their self-respect, their joy in life. How can these things be restored? By pursuing righteousness instead of wealth.

"The blessing of the LORD brings wealth, and he adds no trouble to it" (Proverbs 10:22). Gambling is a wealth that comes with strings attached. The Lord, in contrast, promises not only wealth, but a wealth free from trouble.

"What the wicked dreads will overtake him; what the righteous desire will be granted" (Proverbs 10:24). So much of gambling has to do with desires. It promises and promises but never delivers. Gambling dangles the carrot in front of the gambler at the end of a very long stick. The gambler does not overtake her desires, dread overtakes the gambler. When we pursue righteousness, however, God grants the desires that spring forth.

The Reality of Wealth

"Wealth is worthless in the day of wrath, but righteousness delivers from death" (Proverbs 11:4). It is certainly true there are no moving vans behind hearses. All the wealth in the world will not add a single day to the time God has given us. It is God who determines when we die, not all the technology or modern science that money can buy. God alone has the power to deliver us from the wrath of death. If a person is interested in a real return on her investment of time and energy, righteousness, not wealth, is the wise bet.

"The house of the righteous contains great treasure, but the income of the wicked brings them trouble" (Proverbs 15:6). God stands ready to fill your house with great treasure, if you will only seek his kingdom and his righteousness. When you set up money as an idol and worship it through gambling, God promises that any income you receive will bring you trouble. This trouble is not a punishment from God but a natural consequence of the way in which you have chosen to fulfill your needs. God wants you to choose him so he can give you the treasures, here and in heaven, that he has prepared for you. He wants to give you the riches of his grace.

The wisdom of Solomon in Ecclesiastes ends this way: "Now all has been heard; here is the conclusion of the matter: Fear God and keep his commandments, for this is the whole duty of man. For God will bring every deed into judgment, including every hidden thing, whether it is good or evil" (Ecclesiastes 12:13-14).

Your gambling and your attitudes about gambling are important to God. Gambling is not a neutral activity. Your gambling tells God what you think of him and what you think of yourself. If gambling has taken on an inappropriate importance in your life, it is time to evaluate, confess, and change. God grieves when we prefer the myths of this world to the reality of his love. He calls us to truth, not myth, and that truth will set us free.

How the Church Can Help Someone Who Gambles

The church, the body of Christ, exists to share God's love with the world around us. We also exist to help our brothers and sisters in the family of faith. The church can provide the necessary reinforcement for Christians' battles with gambling. As a caring family, the church needs to be alert to the signs of gambling, active in reaching out to those caught in gambling's trap, and loving in its response to those in need.

The difficulty in providing this help is the secret nature of compulsive gambling. Very few Christians who gamble admit their behavior to others. They may be open regarding their need for money but closed about the reasons for their financial difficulties. Because of this, an ongoing need for money may be the first clue a church leader has that someone has a problem with gambling.

Churches are known as loving, giving institutions where people are forgiven and accepted. This leads to some misconceptions about the church and money. Some people feel the church should give to all in need and should allow the individual to define what constitutes that need. Most churches and benevolence ministries are aware of this misconception and counter it this way: Churches should give to people in need but be wise about what that need really is. No matter what the physical need, all who ask for help have spiritual needs. Church leaders need to separate the physical need from the spiritual and help people who want money to deal also with their spiritual poverty.

PICKING UP THE PIECES

Compulsive gamblers are often not the people who first contact the church for help. If the gambler is married, usually the spouse makes the first contact. With a partner off pursuing a love for gambling, the spouse is left to pick up the family and the financial pieces. This task can be overwhelming, and those connected with a spiritual family may decide to seek help from the church.

This is usually not a step taken lightly but one fueled by desperation. The spouse will have tried everything she can think of to change the loved one's gambling behavior. When everything fails, her desperation will outweigh the desire to keep her troubles private.

Why would someone in trouble keep that trouble secret? The answer is simple: shame. Opening up your problems to others can produce overwhelming feelings of shame. It's shameful to admit your family is in trouble. It's shameful to admit your spouse doesn't love you enough to stop gambling. It's shameful to admit you're a failure. Bills need to be paid and many people feel it's shameful to ask for money. They feel so much shame, it's painful.

As a church leader, remember that gambling affects the entire family. The call for help comes on behalf of the gambler, but there may be a spouse and children who will need to be ministered to also. It may be a teenager who is gambling, but parents and siblings need care and compassion too. Whenever a family member becomes involved in compulsive gambling, the entire family is strained. Each member of the family needs to be loved.

WHEN THE GAMBLER IS UNKNOWN

The sad reality is that many times the gambler will be a stranger to the leadership at the church. Either he has only come sporadically, or his gambling has kept him from participating in church activities altogether. It may be that the strain of gambling on the family has caused the spouse to become involved in a church and the gambler has never become involved.

In any of these scenarios, the gambler will be a stranger or a relative stranger to the church leaders who are called to minister to him. Ministering is extremely difficult if there is no foundational relationship. This difficulty will be compounded if the gambler is in denial regarding his behavior. Quite simply, the gambler may refuse any help from the leaders of the church. This does not mean, however, that help cannot be offered.

Even if the gambler refuses to be ministered to, the church leaders can pray. Pray for a change of heart. Pray for the gambler to be broken. Pray for God to send someone who does have a relationship with the gambler to deliver the truth. Pray for patience, wisdom, and guidance.

Regardless of whether the gambler is willing to participate, if a family is involved, many people should minister to the entire family. The church leadership group can work with the family as a whole, but the husband and wife may need someone who can assist with marital issues that may arise because of the gambling. The children may need a safe home away from home, where they can go when the tensions of the family become too great or when the husband and wife need time alone to work through difficult issues.

If the gambler refuses to participate, the other members of the family will still need to be ministered to. As the family situation deteriorates because of the gambling, the remaining spouse and the children may need help finding an alternative living arrangement. At some point, the unrepentant gambler may rebuff all efforts to curtail his gambling by leaving the family. This is a tragic possibility, especially if the gambler has no connection to the church.

There is always hope, of course, that the gambler will see the way the church is ministering to the family and decide to trust the leaders and seek help. In this case, the church leaders should be open to the leading of the Spirit as to which of the leaders, or perhaps someone else, would be best to work with the gambler. God knows the gambler, and he knows the people in the church. Certainly the whole leadership can meet with the gambler and his family, but there should be someone who is a primary support person.

That contact person should be chosen carefully. It should be someone who will be able to forge common ground with the gambler. Perhaps someone in a similar line of work or from the same part of the country. It should be someone who is able to handle the commitment of ministering to the gambler, whenever that time may be. Because of this, the leader should be someone who has time to give, perhaps retired or with a flexible job situation. It should be someone who is mature in the faith. The issues surrounding gambling are complex, highly personal, and spiritually challenging. The leader should be a mature Christian, wise in speech, and a good listener.

When the Gambler Is Known

In some cases the gambler may be well known to the leaders of the church. He may be the last person the leaders would suspect of having a problem. If the gambler is known to the church, that relationship can be a beginning point for healing.

Gambling will have undoubtedly weakened the gambler's relationship to the church. The gambler may have withdrawn from fellowship in order to spend more time gambling. He may have withdrawn because of feelings of shame or guilt about his gambling. By the time the gambling behavior is noticed by the church leadership, he may have had little or no contact with the church for months or even years.

If the gambler is not part of a family group and has withdrawn from the church, it can be difficult to recognize gambling, at first, as the source of the estrangement. The church leaders will need to seek out this person and try to determine why he has left the church. All they can do is ask. The gambler may or may not answer honestly. In some cases, the circumstances may provide the answer. If the gambler becomes desperate for money, having depleted all other sources of cash, he might decide to recontact the church or individual church members. If the gambler is still in possession of a church directory, he may begin to go through the list of members, asking for money.

A Plan for Healing

Whether the gambler is known or unknown in the church, when gambling has been identified as the source of the problem, church leaders need to do the following:

1. Pray for the gambler, any family members, and for themselves. This is first and foremost in any plan for ministry. A gambling compulsion is larger and stronger than an individual's will. The strength for healing and redemption can only come through God's power. The wisdom to know how to respond to the gambler's needs can only be given by God. Prayer is the conduit through which his strength, wisdom, and power can flow.

2. If the gambler is willing to change, be firm and unmistakable that any help from the church will only come when he stops gambling. The leadership should craft a way to know whether the gambler's commitment to stop is honored. Ideally, the spouse should not be the one who has to do this monitoring because there is enough strain on the marriage due to gambling without the nongambling spouse becoming the "gambling

police." (Also, the nongambling spouse has probably already tried this without success.) Instead, one of the leaders should agree to work with the gambler to monitor his progress.

3. If the gambler is unwilling to change, the church should give assistance only to the other family members but never in the form of cash. This help can come in the way of food for the family or pledges toward utilities or rent. At some point, however, the church will not be able to support the family's living expenses. The church and family may need to pray and plan for the family and the gambler to be separated.

4. Strongly consider helping to pay for professional counseling for the gambler and family. Gambling has a way of covering up a wide variety of destructive issues. When gambling is challenged, those issues may rise to the surface. Dealing with those issues may take a professional setting. With funds already strained because of the gambling, the family may need to access church funds to pay for the services of a competent Christian counselor. If this financial burden is too great, assist the gambler in contacting and attending a support group such as Gamblers Anonymous.

5. Be prepared to remain actively involved in ministering to the gambler and family for the long haul. Recovery from an addiction can be months or years in the making. Church leaders will need to have perseverance to stay connected to the gambler and to the family during this process.

6. Support and encourage the members of the ministry team. When many people are ministering to the gambler and family, it is important for all of those people to operate as a team, not as independent players. All those ministering will need to commit to a regular time of communication with each other to ensure that the messages being delivered to the gambler, the spouse (or parents), and the children (or siblings) are compatible with each

other. Getting together to coordinate the ministry to this family will allow the leaders to pray together for the family as well.

Perhaps the most important thing for you to do as a church leader is to be transparent to those you serve in the church. Your transparency will help you to be accessible to the people in the church who need your help. Too often when people are in trouble, the church is the last place they would dream of going for help. They expect to find condemnation there instead. When church leaders appear just a little too perfect, they seem unapproachable.

Those around you need to know the struggles you are having, how you are dealing with those struggles, and how your faith in God factors into your struggles and your victories. They need to know that though you sin, you receive God's forgiveness. If you are forgiven, they may be more able to hope that they can be forgiven too.

As a church leader, it is not your job to have the answer to every problem. That would be redundant, because God already knows both the problem and the solution. Your job is to be so in tune with God that he is able to reveal to you what the problem and the solutions are. Keep reading Scripture. Remain open to what God is teaching you about difficult situations like gambling. Some of the scriptures and issues addressed in this book may be a place to start.

May God fill you with his wisdom, strength, and power as you minister to those in your care. May he provide you with insight, compassion, and grace.

GAMBLING PERSONALITY QUESTIONNAIRE

At any point in your reading of this book, you are encouraged to ask yourself the questions below. The questions are designed to cause you to think about and evaluate your gambling behaviors or the gambling behaviors of someone you care about. As mentioned before, it might be helpful to take this test at several points during your reading of the book. Your answers may change the more you read. You may use this as a personal inventory, as discussed in chapter 12.

There are no right or wrong answers to this questionnaire. There is no formula that states you do or don't have a problem with gambling if you answer yes to this or that many questions. The final decision about whether gambling has become a problem is ultimately up to you and God.

Before you answer these questions, spend some time in prayer asking God to reveal his will through your responses. Ask him to test your heart, as David did: "Search me, O God, and know my heart; test me and know my anxious thoughts. See if there be any offensive way in me, and lead me in the way everlasting" (Psalm 139:23-24).

Acknowledging our ways as offensive to God is not easy, but God stands ready to remedy even the condition of our hearts. Listen to what the Lord says in Ezekiel: "I will give you a new heart and put a new spirit in you; I will remove from you your heart of stone and give you a heart of flesh. And I will put my Spirit in you and move you to follow my decrees and be careful to keep my laws" (Ezekiel 36:26-27). Our hearts must be open to God and honest to ourselves. Then God can give us a new heart and empower us to change.

Answer these questions honestly and open your heart to God.

1. Consider the things in your life of value to you. They can include family and friends, activities you enjoy or find meaningful. How much time do you devote to each of these valuable things?

2. How much time do you devote to gambling during a week? Contrast that amount of time with the time you put down for the valuable things in your life.

3. Think about how you feel when you gamble. Are those feelings negative or positive? If they are negative, consider why you engage in an activity that promotes negative feelings. If they are positive, how long do those positive feelings last? Do they outlast the gambling activity itself, or do they dissipate as soon as you have stopped gambling?

4. With busy lives, often decisions must be made about how to spend our time. Think back over the past six months. How many times has a decision about whether to gamble come up against a need to do another activity? This could be time spent with family or friends, time spent working, even time spent relaxing or sleeping. How often has gambling won out over these other things and at what cost?

5. When you think back over your gambling, does it seem like you enjoyed it more at the beginning or now? If it has changed over time, can you remember when the transition occurred?

6. Do you feel isolated from your family or friends when you gamble? Do you feel as if they are unable to understand the way you feel about it? If they are out of touch with gambling, do you feel they are out of touch with you?

7. When other people have questioned you about your gambling, how have you felt? Do you feel they are invading your privacy by questioning you? Do you feel defensive about your gambling?

8. How honest have you been with others about how much time you spend gambling and/or how much money you spend gambling? Do you find yourself trying to hide or cover up the truth about your gambling?

9. When you are in the midst of gambling, do you ever feel like you are "getting away" with something? How does that make you feel? Bad? Excited?

10. Consider your gambling over the past six months. Now consider your spirituality over the past six months. Has your gambling increased and your spirituality decreased? Have you missed your connection with God? Would you be willing to alter your gambling behavior if it meant being closer to God?

11. Think about all of the things gambling promises. Honestly evaluate how much of a motivation those things are in your life. Do you desire them too much? Is gambling really the way to achieve them?

12. When you are gambling, do you engage in activities you feel guilty about? Do you drink or smoke excessively while gambling? Do you flirt or engage in sexual conversations with other gamblers? Does gambling strengthen your resolve to live a godly life or does it weaken you?

13. If you had to give up gambling or your loved ones tomorrow, which would you choose? Having chosen to give up the first thing—gambling—did you still wish you could somehow continue to have both? Were you relieved it was only a question and not a reality?

14. If you had to give up gambling or God tomorrow, which one would you choose? Have you made this choice already?

A MORE SYSTEMATIC APPROACH

It can be difficult to study our behavior and our heart. So often we choose activities to numb or mask what we're really feeling. We get busy so we never have to stop long enough and really look at ourselves. The previous questions were designed to allow you to stop, pray, and look at yourself with God's help. Your responses are yours and God's to evaluate.

Some people, however, like a more systematic approach. They are more comfortable with behaviors than feelings. Knowing this, the following twenty questions are provided. They are the twenty questions used by Gamblers Anonymous to indicate a problem with gambling. According to their material, most compulsive gamblers will answer yes to at least seven of the following questions. (Be aware, however, that even if you answer yes to only four or three or two or five, you may not be "right" in God's sight. God is a jealous God and may have a different standard where you are concerned than Gamblers Anonymous does! Each person has a unique, individual relationship with God, and only he knows our heart and our weaknesses.)

1. Did you ever lose time from work or school due to gambling?
2. Has gambling ever made your home life unhappy?
3. Did gambling ever affect your reputation?
4. Have you ever had remorse after gambling?
5. Did you ever gamble to get money with which to pay debts or otherwise solve financial difficulties?
6. Did gambling cause a decrease in your ambition or efficiency?
7. After losing, did you feel you must return as soon as possible and win back your loses?
8. After a win, did you have a strong urge to return and win more?
9. Did you often gamble until your last dollar was gone?
10. Did you ever borrow to finance your gambling?
11. Have you ever sold anything to finance your gambling?

12. Were you reluctant to use "gambling money" for normal expenditures?

13. Did gambling make you careless of the welfare of yourself or your family?

14. Did you ever gamble longer than you had planned?

15. Have you ever gambled to escape worry or trouble?

16. Have you ever committed, or considered committing, an illegal act to finance gambling?

17. Did gambling cause you to have difficulty in sleeping?

18. Do arguments, disappointments, or frustrations create within you an urge to gamble?

19. Did you ever have an urge to celebrate any good fortune by a few hours of gambling?

20. Have you ever considered self-destruction or suicide as a result of your gambling?

Out-of-control gambling is serious. For you, even moderate gambling may be serious enough that you will need to stop. Any activity that compromises your commitment to God, weakens your relationships with those you love, tempts you into additional sin, and clouds your view of the truth is serious and needs to be taken seriously.

May God bless your decision to look courageously upon your life and evaluate your heart. May he, to his glory, create in you a new heart and renew a right spirit within you.

Appendix D

Gambling Help Lines

A number of helpful resources are available to gamblers and their families:

Compulsive Gambling Center: 924 E. Baltimore Street; Baltimore, MD 21202; (410) 332-1111

Gam-Anon: P.O. Box 157; Whitestone, NY 11357; (718) 352-1671
Gam-Anon is a nationwide support group for those whose spouse, friend, or family member has a gambling problem.

Gamblers Anonymous: P.O. Box 17173; Los Angeles, CA 90017; (213) 386-8789
Gamblers Anonymous is a twelve-step program for people who struggle with gambling. Call this number to find out about support groups and programs in your area.

Gamblers Helpline: 1-800-994-0899
This help line will provide useful information for gamblers and their family.

National Council on Problem Gambling: 445 W. 59th Street, Room 1521; New York, NY 10019; (212) 765-3833

National Gambling Council Helpline: 1-800-522-4700
Each state has an individual gambling council. This help line can give you information about your state's council and provide information and referrals to Gamblers Anonymous groups and to counselors who specialize in gambling problems.

Notes

Introduction

1. National Gambling Impact Study Commission Report (NGISC), 18 June 1999, 2.
2. Barna Research Group (www.barna.org).
3. Howard J. Schaeffer, Matthew N. Hall, Toni Vanderbilt, "Estimating the Prevalence of Disordered Gambling Behavior in the United States and Canada: A Meta-Analysis," Harvard Medical School Division of Addictions, 15 December 1997, 51.
4. NGISC Executive Summary, 17.

Section 1: The Hand That Rolls the Dice

1. National Opinion Research Center study for the National Gambling Impact Study Commission, 25.

Chapter 1: Just for Thrills

1. Channing L. Bete Company, Inc., "About Gambling Problems," 1999 ed., 6, included in materials provided by the Washington State Council on Problem Gambling.
2. Frank Farley, "The Big T in Personality," *Psychology Today* (May 1986): 47.
3. Farley, "The Big T in Personality," 46.

Chapter 2: For the Love of Money

1. National Gambling Impact Study Commission Report (NGISC), 18 June 1999, 4.
2. NGISC, 4.
3. Analysis of the Casino Survey by the National Opinion Research Center at the University of Chicago for NGISC, 14 April 1999, 5.
4. Robert A. Reno, "The National Gambling Impact Study Commission Report: What Does It Say? What Does It Mean?" Focus on the Family

Research, 10 September 1999, pt. 2, 5 (http://www.family.org/cforum/research/papers/a0007725.html).

5. Reno, "The National Gambling Impact Study Commission Report." 5.

6. Reno, "The National Gambling Impact Study Commission Report," 5.

7. Channing L. Bete Company, Inc., "About Gambling Problems," 1999 ed., 6, included in materials provided by the Washington State Council on Problem Gambling.

8. NGISC, 14.

9. NGISC, Summary Statement by Commissioner James C. Dobson, 2.

10. Reno, "The National Gambling Impact Study Commission Report," pt. 2, 9.

Chapter 5: The Comfort Payoff

1. Erika Gosker, *The Elder Law Journal* (University of Illinois College of Law at Urbana-Champaign) (October 1999), quoted in Carole Fleck, "Are Casinos Preying on Our Elders?" *AARP Magazine* (March 2000).

2. Fleck, "Are Casinos Preying on Our Elders?" 11.

3. National Gambling Impact Study Commission, Summary Statement by Commissioner James C. Dobson, 1.

Chapter 6: The Next Generation

1. Rachel A. Volberg and W. Lamar Moore, "Gambling and Problem Gambling Among Adolescents in Washington State: A Replication Study, 1993 to 1999, Report to the Washington State Lottery," Executive Summary Findings, vii.

2. Volberg and Moore, "Gambling and Problem Gambling Among Adolescents," vii.

3. National Gambling Impact Study Commission Report (NGISC), 18 June 1999, 7-20.

4. NGISC, Summary Statement by Commissioner James C. Dobson, 1.

5. NGISC, Summary Statement, 1.

6. News release, "Focus on the Family Urges McDonald's to Withdraw Lottery Promotion," 22 September 1998.

7. Robert A. Reno, "The National Gambling Impact Study Commission Report: What Does It Say? What Does It Mean?" Focus on the Family Research, 10 September 1999, pt. 2, 2 (http://www.family.org/cforum/research/papers/a0007725.html).

8. Volberg and Moore, "Gambling and Problem Gambling Among Adolescents," vii.
9. Statistics from the National Council on Problem Gambling, quoted in Robert R. Perkinson, "Teenage Gambling," *Professional Counselor Magazine* (December 1999): 13-4.
10. Howard J. Shaffer and Matthew N. Hall, "Estimating the Prevalence of Adolescent Gambling Disorders: A Quantitative Synthesis and Guide Toward Standard Gambling Nomenclature," *Journal of Gambling Studies* (Summer 1996): 193.
11. Volberg and Moore, "Gambling and Problem Gambling Among Adolescents," vii-viii.
12. NGISC, 6.
13. Statistics from the American Academy of Pediatrics, quoted in Robert R. Perkinson, "Teenage Gambling," *Professional Counselor Magazine* (December 1999): 11.
14. Statistics from the American Academy of Pediatrics, quoted in Perkinson, "Teenage Gambling," 11.

Section 2: When Culture Raises the Stakes

1. National Gambling Impact Study Commission Report (NGISC), 18 June 1999, 1.

Chapter 7: Bright Nights, Dark Days

1. National Gambling Impact Study Commission Report (NGISC), 18 June 1999, 4-5.
2. NGISC, 4-5.
3. NGISC, 5.
4. NGISC, 4-5.
5. Robert A. Reno, "The National Gambling Impact Study Commission Report: What Does It Say? What Does It Mean?" Focus on the Family Research, 10 September 1999, pt. 2, 10 (http://www.family.org/cforum/research/papers/a0007725.html).
6. Reno, "The National Gambling Impact Study Commission Report," pt. 2, 9.
7. NGISC, 28.
8. Reno, "The National Gambling Impact Study Commission Report," pt. 4, 4. (http://www.family.org/cforum/research/papers/a0007727.html)

9. NGISC, 6.
10. NGISC, 6.
11. NGISC, 6, 18-20.
12. Reno, "The National Gambling Impact Study Commission Report," pt. 3, 1-3 (http://www.family.org/cforum/research/papers/a0007726.html).
13. NGISC, 7.
14. NGISC, 20.
15. NGISC, Recommendations, chap. 5, Recommendations 5-1, 5-2.
16. NGISC, Recommendations, chap. 5, Recommendations 5-1, 5-2.
17. Testimony of Tom W. Bell, director, Telecommunications and Technology Studies at the Cato Institute, before the NGISC, Chicago, Ill., 21 May 1998.
18. NGISC, 21.
19. NGISC, 21.
20. Reno, "The National Gambling Impact Study Commission Report," pt. 1, 5 (http://www.family.org/cforum/research/papers/a0007724.html).

Chapter 8: Just a Little Wager

1. Rachel A. Volberg and W. Lamar Moore, "Gambling and Problem Gambling Among Adolescents in Washington State: A Replication Study, 1993 to 1999, Report to the Washington State Lottery," Executive Summary Findings, vii.
2. Howard Chua-Eoan and Tim Larimer, "The Poké Mania," *Time,* 22 November 1999, 84.
3. Volberg and Moore, "Gambling and Problem Gambling Among Adolescents," viii.

Chapter 9: When One Thing Leads to Another

1. National Gambling Impact Study Commission Report (NGISC), 18 June 1999, Summary Statement by Commissioner James C. Dobson, 2.
2. NGISC, Recommendations, chap. 8, Recommendations 8-20.
3. Robert R. Perkinson, "Teenage Gambling," *Professional Counselor Magazine* (December 1999): 14.
4. Robert A. Reno, "Gambling and Crime," Focus on the Family Research, 27 December 1999, 1 (http://www.family.org/cforum/research/papers/a0000928.html).

5. Rachel A. Volberg and W. Lamar Moore, "Gambling and Problem Gambling Among Adolescents in Washington State: A Replication Study, 1993 to 1999, Report to the Washington State Lottery," Executive Summary Findings, vii.

6. Volberg and Moore, "Gambling and Problem Gambling Among Adolescents," viii.

7. American Psychological Association, APA Public Communications (http://www.apa.org/releases/internet.html).

8. For further information regarding addictive behaviors and the Internet, see Gregory L. Jantz and Ann McMurray, *Hidden Dangers of the Internet* (Colorado Springs, Colo.: Shaw, 1998).

Chapter 10: Evangelical Consumerism

1. Athena Dean, *Consumed by Success: Reaching the Top and Finding God Wasn't There* (Mukilteo, Wash.: WinePress Publishing, 1996), 44.

2. Dean, *Consumed by Success*, 25.

3. Bradley Orner, "Amway: The Untold Story" (http://www.newwave.net/poohbear/aus/stats.htm).

Chapter 11: When the Luck Runs Out

1. Louis A. Cobarruvias, City of San Jose, Calif., memorandum from the chief of police to the mayor and the city council, 27 October 1995.

2. Robert A. Reno, "Gambling and Crime," Focus on the Family Research, 27 December 1999 (http://www.family.org/cforum/research/papers/a0000928.html).

3. Andrew J. Buck, Simon Hakim, and Uriel Spiegel, "Casinos, Crime and Real Estate Values: Do They Relate?" *Journal of Research in Crime and Delinquency* (August 1991): 295.

4. Mayor Wesley J. Johnson Sr., "Fiscal Impacts of the Foxwoods Casino on the Town of Ledyard, Connecticut," April 1997.

5. J. Joseph Curran Jr., "The House Never Loses and Maryland Cannot Win: Why Casino Gambling Is a Bad Idea," Report of Attorney General J. Joseph Curran Jr. on the impact of casino gambling on crime, 16 October 1995, 9.

6. William N. Thompson, Ricardo Gazel, and Dan Rickman, "Casinos and Crime in Wisconsin: What's the Connection?" *Wisconsin Policy Research Institute Report*, November 1996.

7. Robert A. Reno, "The National Gambling Impact Study Commission Report: What Does It Say? What Does It Mean?" Focus on the Family Research, 10 September 1999, pt. 1, 5 (http://www.family.org/cforum/research/papers/a0007724.html).

8. Reno, "The National Gambling Impact Study Commission Report," pt. 1, 6.

9. As reported in Robert R. Perkinson, "Teenage Gambling," *Professional Counselor Magazine* (December 1999): 14.

10. John Hoffman et al., "Analysis of the Casino Survey: Report to the National Gambling Impact Study Commission," National Opinion Research Center at the University of Chicago, 14 April 1999, 5.

11. National Gambling Impact Study Commission Report (NGISC), 18 June 1999, Executive Summary, Recommendation 7:1, 39.

12. Reno, "The National Gambling Impact Study Commission Report," pt.1, 9.

13. Reno, "The National Gambling Impact Study Commission Report," pt. 1, 9.

14. Washington State Council on Problem Gambling brochure.

15. NGISC, 17.

16. Reno, "The National Gambling Impact Study Commission Report," pt. 1, 10.

17. Reno, "The National Gambling Impact Study Commission Report," pt. 1, 11.

18. Reno, "The National Gambling Impact Study Commission Report," pt. 1, 9.

19. According to information provided by the Washington State Council on Problem Gambling, unemployment for problem gamblers is twice that of the general population, and those who do work are less productive.

20. Reno, "The National Gambling Impact Study Commission Report," pt. 1, 8.

21. Reno, "The National Gambling Impact Study Commission Report," pt. 1, 8.

22. Reno, "The National Gambling Impact Study Commission Report," pt. 1, 8.

23. Perkinson, "Teenage Gambling," 13-4; statistics quoted from the National Council on Problem Gambling.

24. Perkinson, "Teenage Gambling," 14.

25. NGISC, 18.

26. NGISC, 2.

Chapter 15: The Source of Hope

1. A wonderful book on this subject is Philip Yancey, *What's So Amazing About Grace?* (Grand Rapids, Mich.: Zondervan, 1997). Provocative and challenging, this book will ask you to look at God, yourself, and others more honestly.

About the Authors

Gregory Jantz, Ph.D., is a popular speaker, author, and host of a daily radio program. He is the founder and executive director of The Center for Counseling and Health Resources, Inc., a leading mental-health and chemical-dependency treatment facility with three clinics in the Seattle area. The center is known as "A Place of Hope." Dr. Jantz and his wife, LaFon, direct a diverse offering of treatment programs in Washington.

Dr. Jantz's "whole person" approach to mental health addresses the emotional, physical, intellectual, relational, and spiritual dimensions of human beings. He has written eight books, including *Hope, Help and Healing for Eating Disorders; Losing Weight Permanently: Secrets of the 2% Who Succeed;* and *Hidden Dangers of the Internet: Using It Without Abusing It.*

For more information, call or write:

The Center for Counseling and Health Resources, Inc.

P.O. Box 700

Edmonds, WA 98020

1-888-771-5166

www.aplaceofhope.com

Ann McMurray is a freelance writer who has worked with Dr. Jantz on several projects, including *Healing the Scars of Emotional Abuse, Hidden Dangers of the Internet: Using It Without Abusing It,* and *Too Close to the Flame: Recognizing and Avoiding Sexualized Relationships.*